C-890   CAREER EXAMINATION SERIES

This is your
PASSBOOK for...

Warehouseman

Test Preparation Study Guide
Questions & Answers

COPYRIGHT NOTICE

This book is SOLELY intended for, is sold ONLY to, and its use is RESTRICTED to individual, bona fide applicants or candidates who qualify by virtue of having seriously filed applications for appropriate license, certificate, professional and/or promotional advancement, higher school matriculation, scholarship, or other legitimate requirements of education and/or governmental authorities.

This book is NOT intended for use, class instruction, tutoring, training, duplication, copying, reprinting, excerption, or adaptation, etc., by:

1) Other publishers
2) Proprietors and/or Instructors of "Coaching" and/or Preparatory Courses
3) Personnel and/or Training Divisions of commercial, industrial, and governmental organizations
4) Schools, colleges, or universities and/or their departments and staffs, including teachers and other personnel
5) Testing Agencies or Bureaus
6) Study groups which seek by the purchase of a single volume to copy and/or duplicate and/or adapt this material for use by the group as a whole without having purchased individual volumes for each of the members of the group
7) Et al.

Such persons would be in violation of appropriate Federal and State statutes.

PROVISION OF LICENSING AGREEMENTS – Recognized educational, commercial, industrial, and governmental institutions and organizations, and others legitimately engaged in educational pursuits, including training, testing, and measurement activities, may address request for a licensing agreement to the copyright owners, who will determine whether, and under what conditions, including fees and charges, the materials in this book may be used them. In other words, a licensing facility exists for the legitimate use of the material in this book on other than an individual basis. However, it is asseverated and affirmed here that the material in this book CANNOT be used without the receipt of the express permission of such a licensing agreement from the Publishers. Inquiries re licensing should be addressed to the company, attention rights and permissions department.

All rights reserved, including the right of reproduction in whole or in part, in any form or by any means, electronic or mechanical, including photocopying, recording, or by any information storage and retrieval system, without permission in writing from the Publisher.

Copyright © 2025 by
National Learning Corporation

212 Michael Drive, Syosset, NY 11791
(516) 921-8888 • www.passbooks.com
E-mail: info@passbooks.com

PASSBOOK® SERIES

THE *PASSBOOK® SERIES* has been created to prepare applicants and candidates for the ultimate academic battlefield – the examination room.

At some time in our lives, each and every one of us may be required to take an examination – for validation, matriculation, admission, qualification, registration, certification, or licensure.

Based on the assumption that every applicant or candidate has met the basic formal educational standards, has taken the required number of courses, and read the necessary texts, the *PASSBOOK® SERIES* furnishes the one special preparation which may assure passing with confidence, instead of failing with insecurity. Examination questions – together with answers – are furnished as the basic vehicle for study so that the mysteries of the examination and its compounding difficulties may be eliminated or diminished by a sure method.

This book is meant to help you pass your examination provided that you qualify and are serious in your objective.

The entire field is reviewed through the huge store of content information which is succinctly presented through a provocative and challenging approach – the question-and-answer method.

A climate of success is established by furnishing the correct answers at the end of each test.

You soon learn to recognize types of questions, forms of questions, and patterns of questioning. You may even begin to anticipate expected outcomes.

You perceive that many questions are repeated or adapted so that you can gain acute insights, which may enable you to score many sure points.

You learn how to confront new questions, or types of questions, and to attack them confidently and work out the correct answers.

You note objectives and emphases, and recognize pitfalls and dangers, so that you may make positive educational adjustments.

Moreover, you are kept fully informed in relation to new concepts, methods, practices, and directions in the field.

You discover that you are actually taking the examination all the time: you are preparing for the examination by "taking" an examination, not by reading extraneous and/or supererogatory textbooks.

In short, this PASSBOOK®, used directedly, should be an important factor in helping you to pass your test.

WAREHOUSEMAN

DUTIES
Performs shipping, stock and storage duties in a large warehouse, receiving and distributing supplies and equipment; performs related duties as required.

SUBJECT OF EXAMINATION
The written test will be designed to test for knowledge, skills, and/or abilities in such areas as:
1. Name and number checking;
2. Keeping simple inventory records;
3. Arithmetic computations;
4. Invoice checking;
5. Storekeeping and inventory control; and
6. Supervision.

HOW TO TAKE A TEST

I. YOU MUST PASS AN EXAMINATION

A. WHAT EVERY CANDIDATE SHOULD KNOW

Examination applicants often ask us for help in preparing for the written test. What can I study in advance? What kinds of questions will be asked? How will the test be given? How will the papers be graded?

As an applicant for a civil service examination, you may be wondering about some of these things. Our purpose here is to suggest effective methods of advance study and to describe civil service examinations.

Your chances for success on this examination can be increased if you know how to prepare. Those "pre-examination jitters" can be reduced if you know what to expect. You can even experience an adventure in good citizenship if you know why civil service exams are given.

B. WHY ARE CIVIL SERVICE EXAMINATIONS GIVEN?

Civil service examinations are important to you in two ways. As a citizen, you want public jobs filled by employees who know how to do their work. As a job seeker, you want a fair chance to compete for that job on an equal footing with other candidates. The best-known means of accomplishing this two-fold goal is the competitive examination.

Exams are widely publicized throughout the nation. They may be administered for jobs in federal, state, city, municipal, town or village governments or agencies.

Any citizen may apply, with some limitations, such as the age or residence of applicants. Your experience and education may be reviewed to see whether you meet the requirements for the particular examination. When these requirements exist, they are reasonable and applied consistently to all applicants. Thus, a competitive examination may cause you some uneasiness now, but it is your privilege and safeguard.

C. HOW ARE CIVIL SERVICE EXAMS DEVELOPED?

Examinations are carefully written by trained technicians who are specialists in the field known as "psychological measurement," in consultation with recognized authorities in the field of work that the test will cover. These experts recommend the subject matter areas or skills to be tested; only those knowledges or skills important to your success on the job are included. The most reliable books and source materials available are used as references. Together, the experts and technicians judge the difficulty level of the questions.

Test technicians know how to phrase questions so that the problem is clearly stated. Their ethics do not permit "trick" or "catch" questions. Questions may have been tried out on sample groups, or subjected to statistical analysis, to determine their usefulness.

Written tests are often used in combination with performance tests, ratings of training and experience, and oral interviews. All of these measures combine to form the best-known means of finding the right person for the right job.

II. HOW TO PASS THE WRITTEN TEST

A. NATURE OF THE EXAMINATION

To prepare intelligently for civil service examinations, you should know how they differ from school examinations you have taken. In school you were assigned certain definite pages to read or subjects to cover. The examination questions were quite detailed and usually emphasized memory. Civil service exams, on the other hand, try to discover your present ability to perform the duties of a position, plus your potentiality to learn these duties. In other words, a civil service exam attempts to predict how successful you will be. Questions cover such a broad area that they cannot be as minute and detailed as school exam questions.

In the public service similar kinds of work, or positions, are grouped together in one "class." This process is known as *position-classification*. All the positions in a class are paid according to the salary range for that class. One class title covers all of these positions, and they are all tested by the same examination.

B. FOUR BASIC STEPS

1) Study the announcement

How, then, can you know what subjects to study? Our best answer is: "Learn as much as possible about the class of positions for which you've applied." The exam will test the knowledge, skills and abilities needed to do the work.

Your most valuable source of information about the position you want is the official exam announcement. This announcement lists the training and experience qualifications. Check these standards and apply only if you come reasonably close to meeting them.

The brief description of the position in the examination announcement offers some clues to the subjects which will be tested. Think about the job itself. Review the duties in your mind. Can you perform them, or are there some in which you are rusty? Fill in the blank spots in your preparation.

Many jurisdictions preview the written test in the exam announcement by including a section called "Knowledge and Abilities Required," "Scope of the Examination," or some similar heading. Here you will find out specifically what fields will be tested.

2) Review your own background

Once you learn in general what the position is all about, and what you need to know to do the work, ask yourself which subjects you already know fairly well and which need improvement. You may wonder whether to concentrate on improving your strong areas or on building some background in your fields of weakness. When the announcement has specified "some knowledge" or "considerable knowledge," or has used adjectives like "beginning principles of…" or "advanced … methods," you can get a clue as to the number and difficulty of questions to be asked in any given field. More questions, and hence broader coverage, would be included for those subjects which are more important in the work. Now weigh your strengths and weaknesses against the job requirements and prepare accordingly.

3) Determine the level of the position

Another way to tell how intensively you should prepare is to understand the level of the job for which you are applying. Is it the entering level? In other words, is this the position in which beginners in a field of work are hired? Or is it an intermediate or advanced level? Sometimes this is indicated by such words as "Junior" or "Senior" in the class title. Other jurisdictions use Roman numerals to designate the level – Clerk I, Clerk II, for example. The word "Supervisor" sometimes appears in the title. If the level is not indicated by the title, check the description of duties. Will you be working under very close supervision, or will you have responsibility for independent decisions in this work?

4) Choose appropriate study materials

Now that you know the subjects to be examined and the relative amount of each subject to be covered, you can choose suitable study materials. For beginning level jobs, or even advanced ones, if you have a pronounced weakness in some aspect of your training, read a modern, standard textbook in that field. Be sure it is up to date and has general coverage. Such books are normally available at your library, and the librarian will be glad to help you locate one. For entry-level positions, questions of appropriate difficulty are chosen – neither highly advanced questions, nor those too simple. Such questions require careful thought but not advanced training.

If the position for which you are applying is technical or advanced, you will read more advanced, specialized material. If you are already familiar with the basic principles of your field, elementary textbooks would waste your time. Concentrate on advanced textbooks and technical periodicals. Think through the concepts and review difficult problems in your field.

These are all general sources. You can get more ideas on your own initiative, following these leads. For example, training manuals and publications of the government agency which employs workers in your field can be useful, particularly for technical and professional positions. A letter or visit to the government department involved may result in more specific study suggestions, and certainly will provide you with a more definite idea of the exact nature of the position you are seeking.

III. KINDS OF TESTS

Tests are used for purposes other than measuring knowledge and ability to perform specified duties. For some positions, it is equally important to test ability to make adjustments to new situations or to profit from training. In others, basic mental abilities not dependent on information are essential. Questions which test these things may not appear as pertinent to the duties of the position as those which test for knowledge and information. Yet they are often highly important parts of a fair examination. For very general questions, it is almost impossible to help you direct your study efforts. What we can do is to point out some of the more common of these general abilities needed in public service positions and describe some typical questions.

1) General information

Broad, general information has been found useful for predicting job success in some kinds of work. This is tested in a variety of ways, from vocabulary lists to questions about current events. Basic background in some field of work, such as sociology or economics, may be sampled in a group of questions. Often these are principles which have become familiar to most persons through exposure rather than through formal training. It is difficult to advise you how to study for these questions; being alert to the world around you is our best suggestion.

2) Verbal ability

An example of an ability needed in many positions is verbal or language ability. Verbal ability is, in brief, the ability to use and understand words. Vocabulary and grammar tests are typical measures of this ability. Reading comprehension or paragraph interpretation questions are common in many kinds of civil service tests. You are given a paragraph of written material and asked to find its central meaning.

3) **Numerical ability**

Number skills can be tested by the familiar arithmetic problem, by checking paired lists of numbers to see which are alike and which are different, or by interpreting charts and graphs. In the latter test, a graph may be printed in the test booklet which you are asked to use as the basis for answering questions.

4) **Observation**

A popular test for law-enforcement positions is the observation test. A picture is shown to you for several minutes, then taken away. Questions about the picture test your ability to observe both details and larger elements.

5) **Following directions**

In many positions in the public service, the employee must be able to carry out written instructions dependably and accurately. You may be given a chart with several columns, each column listing a variety of information. The questions require you to carry out directions involving the information given in the chart.

6) **Skills and aptitudes**

Performance tests effectively measure some manual skills and aptitudes. When the skill is one in which you are trained, such as typing or shorthand, you can practice. These tests are often very much like those given in business school or high school courses. For many of the other skills and aptitudes, however, no short-time preparation can be made. Skills and abilities natural to you or that you have developed throughout your lifetime are being tested.

Many of the general questions just described provide all the data needed to answer the questions and ask you to use your reasoning ability to find the answers. Your best preparation for these tests, as well as for tests of facts and ideas, is to be at your physical and mental best. You, no doubt, have your own methods of getting into an exam-taking mood and keeping "in shape." The next section lists some ideas on this subject.

IV. KINDS OF QUESTIONS

Only rarely is the "essay" question, which you answer in narrative form, used in civil service tests. Civil service tests are usually of the short-answer type. Full instructions for answering these questions will be given to you at the examination. But in case this is your first experience with short-answer questions and separate answer sheets, here is what you need to know:

1) **Multiple-choice Questions**

Most popular of the short-answer questions is the "multiple choice" or "best answer" question. It can be used, for example, to test for factual knowledge, ability to solve problems or judgment in meeting situations found at work.

A multiple-choice question is normally one of three types—
- It can begin with an incomplete statement followed by several possible endings. You are to find the one ending which *best* completes the statement, although some of the others may not be entirely wrong.
- It can also be a complete statement in the form of a question which is answered by choosing one of the statements listed.

- It can be in the form of a problem – again you select the best answer.

Here is an example of a multiple-choice question with a discussion which should give you some clues as to the method for choosing the right answer:

When an employee has a complaint about his assignment, the action which will *best* help him overcome his difficulty is to
- A. discuss his difficulty with his coworkers
- B. take the problem to the head of the organization
- C. take the problem to the person who gave him the assignment
- D. say nothing to anyone about his complaint

In answering this question, you should study each of the choices to find which is best. Consider choice "A" – Certainly an employee may discuss his complaint with fellow employees, but no change or improvement can result, and the complaint remains unresolved. Choice "B" is a poor choice since the head of the organization probably does not know what assignment you have been given, and taking your problem to him is known as "going over the head" of the supervisor. The supervisor, or person who made the assignment, is the person who can clarify it or correct any injustice. Choice "C" is, therefore, correct. To say nothing, as in choice "D," is unwise. Supervisors have and interest in knowing the problems employees are facing, and the employee is seeking a solution to his problem.

2) True/False Questions

The "true/false" or "right/wrong" form of question is sometimes used. Here a complete statement is given. Your job is to decide whether the statement is right or wrong.

SAMPLE: A roaming cell-phone call to a nearby city costs less than a non-roaming call to a distant city.

This statement is wrong, or false, since roaming calls are more expensive.

This is not a complete list of all possible question forms, although most of the others are variations of these common types. You will always get complete directions for answering questions. Be sure you understand *how* to mark your answers – ask questions until you do.

V. RECORDING YOUR ANSWERS

Computer terminals are used more and more today for many different kinds of exams.

For an examination with very few applicants, you may be told to record your answers in the test booklet itself. Separate answer sheets are much more common. If this separate answer sheet is to be scored by machine – and this is often the case – it is highly important that you mark your answers correctly in order to get credit.

An electronic scoring machine is often used in civil service offices because of the speed with which papers can be scored. Machine-scored answer sheets must be marked with a pencil, which will be given to you. This pencil has a high graphite content which responds to the electronic scoring machine. As a matter of fact, stray dots may register as answers, so do not let your pencil rest on the answer sheet while you are pondering the correct answer. Also, if your pencil lead breaks or is otherwise defective, ask for another.

Since the answer sheet will be dropped in a slot in the scoring machine, be careful not to bend the corners or get the paper crumpled.

The answer sheet normally has five vertical columns of numbers, with 30 numbers to a column. These numbers correspond to the question numbers in your test booklet. After each number, going across the page are four or five pairs of dotted lines. These short dotted lines have small letters or numbers above them. The first two pairs may also have a "T" or "F" above the letters. This indicates that the first two pairs only are to be used if the questions are of the true-false type. If the questions are multiple choice, disregard the "T" and "F" and pay attention only to the small letters or numbers.

Answer your questions in the manner of the sample that follows:

    32. The largest city in the United States is
        A. Washington, D.C.
        B. New York City
        C. Chicago
        D. Detroit
        E. San Francisco

1) Choose the answer you think is best. (New York City is the largest, so "B" is correct.)
2) Find the row of dotted lines numbered the same as the question you are answering. (Find row number 32)
3) Find the pair of dotted lines corresponding to the answer. (Find the pair of lines under the mark "B.")
4) Make a solid black mark between the dotted lines.

VI. BEFORE THE TEST

Common sense will help you find procedures to follow to get ready for an examination. Too many of us, however, overlook these sensible measures. Indeed, nervousness and fatigue have been found to be the most serious reasons why applicants fail to do their best on civil service tests. Here is a list of reminders:

- Begin your preparation early – Don't wait until the last minute to go scurrying around for books and materials or to find out what the position is all about.
- Prepare continuously – An hour a night for a week is better than an all-night cram session. This has been definitely established. What is more, a night a week for a month will return better dividends than crowding your study into a shorter period of time.
- Locate the place of the exam – You have been sent a notice telling you when and where to report for the examination. If the location is in a different town or otherwise unfamiliar to you, it would be well to inquire the best route and learn something about the building.
- Relax the night before the test – Allow your mind to rest. Do not study at all that night. Plan some mild recreation or diversion; then go to bed early and get a good night's sleep.
- Get up early enough to make a leisurely trip to the place for the test – This way unforeseen events, traffic snarls, unfamiliar buildings, etc. will not upset you.
- Dress comfortably – A written test is not a fashion show. You will be known by number and not by name, so wear something comfortable.

- Leave excess paraphernalia at home – Shopping bags and odd bundles will get in your way. You need bring only the items mentioned in the official notice you received; usually everything you need is provided. Do not bring reference books to the exam. They will only confuse those last minutes and be taken away from you when in the test room.
- Arrive somewhat ahead of time – If because of transportation schedules you must get there very early, bring a newspaper or magazine to take your mind off yourself while waiting.
- Locate the examination room – When you have found the proper room, you will be directed to the seat or part of the room where you will sit. Sometimes you are given a sheet of instructions to read while you are waiting. Do not fill out any forms until you are told to do so; just read them and be prepared.
- Relax and prepare to listen to the instructions
- If you have any physical problem that may keep you from doing your best, be sure to tell the test administrator. If you are sick or in poor health, you really cannot do your best on the exam. You can come back and take the test some other time.

VII. AT THE TEST

The day of the test is here and you have the test booklet in your hand. The temptation to get going is very strong. Caution! There is more to success than knowing the right answers. You must know how to identify your papers and understand variations in the type of short-answer question used in this particular examination. Follow these suggestions for maximum results from your efforts:

1) Cooperate with the monitor
The test administrator has a duty to create a situation in which you can be as much at ease as possible. He will give instructions, tell you when to begin, check to see that you are marking your answer sheet correctly, and so on. He is not there to guard you, although he will see that your competitors do not take unfair advantage. He wants to help you do your best.

2) Listen to all instructions
Don't jump the gun! Wait until you understand all directions. In most civil service tests you get more time than you need to answer the questions. So don't be in a hurry. Read each word of instructions until you clearly understand the meaning. Study the examples, listen to all announcements and follow directions. Ask questions if you do not understand what to do.

3) Identify your papers
Civil service exams are usually identified by number only. You will be assigned a number; you must not put your name on your test papers. Be sure to copy your number correctly. Since more than one exam may be given, copy your exact examination title.

4) Plan your time
Unless you are told that a test is a "speed" or "rate of work" test, speed itself is usually not important. Time enough to answer all the questions will be provided, but this does not mean that you have all day. An overall time limit has been set. Divide the total time (in minutes) by the number of questions to determine the approximate time you have for each question.

5) Do not linger over difficult questions

If you come across a difficult question, mark it with a paper clip (useful to have along) and come back to it when you have been through the booklet. One caution if you do this – be sure to skip a number on your answer sheet as well. Check often to be sure that you have not lost your place and that you are marking in the row numbered the same as the question you are answering.

6) Read the questions

Be sure you know what the question asks! Many capable people are unsuccessful because they failed to *read* the questions correctly.

7) Answer all questions

Unless you have been instructed that a penalty will be deducted for incorrect answers, it is better to guess than to omit a question.

8) Speed tests

It is often better NOT to guess on speed tests. It has been found that on timed tests people are tempted to spend the last few seconds before time is called in marking answers at random – without even reading them – in the hope of picking up a few extra points. To discourage this practice, the instructions may warn you that your score will be "corrected" for guessing. That is, a penalty will be applied. The incorrect answers will be deducted from the correct ones, or some other penalty formula will be used.

9) Review your answers

If you finish before time is called, go back to the questions you guessed or omitted to give them further thought. Review other answers if you have time.

10) Return your test materials

If you are ready to leave before others have finished or time is called, take ALL your materials to the monitor and leave quietly. Never take any test material with you. The monitor can discover whose papers are not complete, and taking a test booklet may be grounds for disqualification.

VIII. EXAMINATION TECHNIQUES

1) Read the general instructions carefully. These are usually printed on the first page of the exam booklet. As a rule, these instructions refer to the timing of the examination; the fact that you should not start work until the signal and must stop work at a signal, etc. If there are any *special* instructions, such as a choice of questions to be answered, make sure that you note this instruction carefully.

2) When you are ready to start work on the examination, that is as soon as the signal has been given, read the instructions to each question booklet, underline any key words or phrases, such as *least, best, outline, describe* and the like. In this way you will tend to answer as requested rather than discover on reviewing your paper that you *listed without describing*, that you selected the *worst* choice rather than the *best* choice, etc.

3) If the examination is of the objective or multiple-choice type – that is, each question will also give a series of possible answers: A, B, C or D, and you are called upon to select the best answer and write the letter next to that answer on your answer paper – it is advisable to start answering each question in turn. There may be anywhere from 50 to 100 such questions in the three or four hours allotted and you can see how much time would be taken if you read through all the questions before beginning to answer any. Furthermore, if you come across a question or group of questions which you know would be difficult to answer, it would undoubtedly affect your handling of all the other questions.

4) If the examination is of the essay type and contains but a few questions, it is a moot point as to whether you should read all the questions before starting to answer any one. Of course, if you are given a choice – say five out of seven and the like – then it is essential to read all the questions so you can eliminate the two that are most difficult. If, however, you are asked to answer all the questions, there may be danger in trying to answer the easiest one first because you may find that you will spend too much time on it. The best technique is to answer the first question, then proceed to the second, etc.

5) Time your answers. Before the exam begins, write down the time it started, then add the time allowed for the examination and write down the time it must be completed, then divide the time available somewhat as follows:
    - If 3-1/2 hours are allowed, that would be 210 minutes. If you have 80 objective-type questions, that would be an average of 2-1/2 minutes per question. Allow yourself no more than 2 minutes per question, or a total of 160 minutes, which will permit about 50 minutes to review.
    - If for the time allotment of 210 minutes there are 7 essay questions to answer, that would average about 30 minutes a question. Give yourself only 25 minutes per question so that you have about 35 minutes to review.

6) The most important instruction is to *read each question* and make sure you know what is wanted. The second most important instruction is to *time yourself properly* so that you answer every question. The third most important instruction is to *answer every question*. Guess if you have to but include something for each question. Remember that you will receive no credit for a blank and will probably receive some credit if you write something in answer to an essay question. If you guess a letter – say "B" for a multiple-choice question – you may have guessed right. If you leave a blank as an answer to a multiple-choice question, the examiners may respect your feelings but it will not add a point to your score. Some exams may penalize you for wrong answers, so in such cases *only*, you may not want to guess unless you have some basis for your answer.

7) Suggestions
    a. Objective-type questions
        1. Examine the question booklet for proper sequence of pages and questions
        2. Read all instructions carefully
        3. Skip any question which seems too difficult; return to it after all other questions have been answered
        4. Apportion your time properly; do not spend too much time on any single question or group of questions

5. Note and underline key words – *all, most, fewest, least, best, worst, same, opposite*, etc.
6. Pay particular attention to negatives
7. Note unusual option, e.g., unduly long, short, complex, different or similar in content to the body of the question
8. Observe the use of "hedging" words – *probably, may, most likely*, etc.
9. Make sure that your answer is put next to the same number as the question
10. Do not second-guess unless you have good reason to believe the second answer is definitely more correct
11. Cross out original answer if you decide another answer is more accurate; do not erase until you are ready to hand your paper in
12. Answer all questions; guess unless instructed otherwise
13. Leave time for review

b. Essay questions
1. Read each question carefully
2. Determine exactly what is wanted. Underline key words or phrases.
3. Decide on outline or paragraph answer
4. Include many different points and elements unless asked to develop any one or two points or elements
5. Show impartiality by giving pros and cons unless directed to select one side only
6. Make and write down any assumptions you find necessary to answer the questions
7. Watch your English, grammar, punctuation and choice of words
8. Time your answers; don't crowd material

8) Answering the essay question

Most essay questions can be answered by framing the specific response around several key words or ideas. Here are a few such key words or ideas:

M's: manpower, materials, methods, money, management
P's: purpose, program, policy, plan, procedure, practice, problems, pitfalls, personnel, public relations

a. Six basic steps in handling problems:
1. Preliminary plan and background development
2. Collect information, data and facts
3. Analyze and interpret information, data and facts
4. Analyze and develop solutions as well as make recommendations
5. Prepare report and sell recommendations
6. Install recommendations and follow up effectiveness

b. Pitfalls to avoid
1. *Taking things for granted* – A statement of the situation does not necessarily imply that each of the elements is necessarily true; for example, a complaint may be invalid and biased so that all that can be taken for granted is that a complaint has been registered

2. *Considering only one side of a situation* – Wherever possible, indicate several alternatives and then point out the reasons you selected the best one
3. *Failing to indicate follow up* – Whenever your answer indicates action on your part, make certain that you will take proper follow-up action to see how successful your recommendations, procedures or actions turn out to be
4. *Taking too long in answering any single question* – Remember to time your answers properly

IX. AFTER THE TEST

Scoring procedures differ in detail among civil service jurisdictions although the general principles are the same. Whether the papers are hand-scored or graded by machine we have described, they are nearly always graded by number. That is, the person who marks the paper knows only the number – never the name – of the applicant. Not until all the papers have been graded will they be matched with names. If other tests, such as training and experience or oral interview ratings have been given, scores will be combined. Different parts of the examination usually have different weights. For example, the written test might count 60 percent of the final grade, and a rating of training and experience 40 percent. In many jurisdictions, veterans will have a certain number of points added to their grades.

After the final grade has been determined, the names are placed in grade order and an eligible list is established. There are various methods for resolving ties between those who get the same final grade – probably the most common is to place first the name of the person whose application was received first. Job offers are made from the eligible list in the order the names appear on it. You will be notified of your grade and your rank as soon as all these computations have been made. This will be done as rapidly as possible.

People who are found to meet the requirements in the announcement are called "eligibles." Their names are put on a list of eligible candidates. An eligible's chances of getting a job depend on how high he stands on this list and how fast agencies are filling jobs from the list.

When a job is to be filled from a list of eligibles, the agency asks for the names of people on the list of eligibles for that job. When the civil service commission receives this request, it sends to the agency the names of the three people highest on this list. Or, if the job to be filled has specialized requirements, the office sends the agency the names of the top three persons who meet these requirements from the general list.

The appointing officer makes a choice from among the three people whose names were sent to him. If the selected person accepts the appointment, the names of the others are put back on the list to be considered for future openings.

That is the rule in hiring from all kinds of eligible lists, whether they are for typist, carpenter, chemist, or something else. For every vacancy, the appointing officer has his choice of any one of the top three eligibles on the list. This explains why the person whose name is on top of the list sometimes does not get an appointment when some of the persons lower on the list do. If the appointing officer chooses the second or third eligible, the No. 1 eligible does not get a job at once, but stays on the list until he is appointed or the list is terminated.

X. HOW TO PASS THE INTERVIEW TEST

The examination for which you applied requires an oral interview test. You have already taken the written test and you are now being called for the interview test – the final part of the formal examination.

You may think that it is not possible to prepare for an interview test and that there are no procedures to follow during an interview. Our purpose is to point out some things you can do in advance that will help you and some good rules to follow and pitfalls to avoid while you are being interviewed.

What is an interview supposed to test?

The written examination is designed to test the technical knowledge and competence of the candidate; the oral is designed to evaluate intangible qualities, not readily measured otherwise, and to establish a list showing the relative fitness of each candidate – as measured against his competitors – for the position sought. Scoring is not on the basis of "right" and "wrong," but on a sliding scale of values ranging from "not passable" to "outstanding." As a matter of fact, it is possible to achieve a relatively low score without a single "incorrect" answer because of evident weakness in the qualities being measured.

Occasionally, an examination may consist entirely of an oral test – either an individual or a group oral. In such cases, information is sought concerning the technical knowledges and abilities of the candidate, since there has been no written examination for this purpose. More commonly, however, an oral test is used to supplement a written examination.

Who conducts interviews?

The composition of oral boards varies among different jurisdictions. In nearly all, a representative of the personnel department serves as chairman. One of the members of the board may be a representative of the department in which the candidate would work. In some cases, "outside experts" are used, and, frequently, a businessman or some other representative of the general public is asked to serve. Labor and management or other special groups may be represented. The aim is to secure the services of experts in the appropriate field.

However the board is composed, it is a good idea (and not at all improper or unethical) to ascertain in advance of the interview who the members are and what groups they represent. When you are introduced to them, you will have some idea of their backgrounds and interests, and at least you will not stutter and stammer over their names.

What should be done before the interview?

While knowledge about the board members is useful and takes some of the surprise element out of the interview, there is other preparation which is more substantive. It *is* possible to prepare for an oral interview – in several ways:

1) Keep a copy of your application and review it carefully before the interview

This may be the only document before the oral board, and the starting point of the interview. Know what education and experience you have listed there, and the sequence and dates of all of it. Sometimes the board will ask you to review the highlights of your experience for them; you should not have to hem and haw doing it.

2) Study the class specification and the examination announcement

Usually, the oral board has one or both of these to guide them. The qualities, characteristics or knowledges required by the position sought are stated in these documents. They offer valuable clues as to the nature of the oral interview. For example, if the job involves supervisory responsibilities, the announcement will usually indicate that knowledge of modern supervisory methods and the qualifications of the candidate as a supervisor will be tested. If so, you can expect such questions, frequently in the form of a hypothetical situation which you are expected to solve. NEVER go into an oral without knowledge of the duties and responsibilities of the job you seek.

3) Think through each qualification required

Try to visualize the kind of questions you would ask if you were a board member. How well could you answer them? Try especially to appraise your own knowledge and background in each area, *measured against the job sought*, and identify any areas in which you are weak. Be critical and realistic – do not flatter yourself.

4) Do some general reading in areas in which you feel you may be weak

For example, if the job involves supervision and your past experience has NOT, some general reading in supervisory methods and practices, particularly in the field of human relations, might be useful. Do NOT study agency procedures or detailed manuals. The oral board will be testing your understanding and capacity, not your memory.

5) Get a good night's sleep and watch your general health and mental attitude

You will want a clear head at the interview. Take care of a cold or any other minor ailment, and of course, no hangovers.

What should be done on the day of the interview?

Now comes the day of the interview itself. Give yourself plenty of time to get there. Plan to arrive somewhat ahead of the scheduled time, particularly if your appointment is in the fore part of the day. If a previous candidate fails to appear, the board might be ready for you a bit early. By early afternoon an oral board is almost invariably behind schedule if there are many candidates, and you may have to wait. Take along a book or magazine to read, or your application to review, but leave any extraneous material in the waiting room when you go in for your interview. In any event, relax and compose yourself.

The matter of dress is important. The board is forming impressions about you – from your experience, your manners, your attitude, and your appearance. Give your personal appearance careful attention. Dress your best, but not your flashiest. Choose conservative, appropriate clothing, and be sure it is immaculate. This is a business interview, and your appearance should indicate that you regard it as such. Besides, being well groomed and properly dressed will help boost your confidence.

Sooner or later, someone will call your name and escort you into the interview room. *This is it.* From here on you are on your own. It is too late for any more preparation. But remember, you asked for this opportunity to prove your fitness, and you are here because your request was granted.

What happens when you go in?

The usual sequence of events will be as follows: The clerk (who is often the board stenographer) will introduce you to the chairman of the oral board, who will introduce you to the other members of the board. Acknowledge the introductions before you sit down. Do not be surprised if you find a microphone facing you or a stenotypist sitting by. Oral interviews are usually recorded in the event of an appeal or other review.

Usually the chairman of the board will open the interview by reviewing the highlights of your education and work experience from your application – primarily for the benefit of the other members of the board, as well as to get the material into the record. Do not interrupt or comment unless there is an error or significant misinterpretation; if that is the case, do not hesitate. But do not quibble about insignificant matters. Also, he will usually ask you some question about your education, experience or your present job – partly to get you to start talking and to establish the interviewing "rapport." He may start the actual questioning, or turn it over to one of the other members. Frequently, each member undertakes the questioning on a particular area, one in which he is perhaps most competent, so you can expect each member to participate in the examination. Because time is limited, you may also expect some rather abrupt switches in the direction the questioning takes, so do not be upset by it. Normally, a board member will not pursue a single line of questioning unless he discovers a particular strength or weakness.

After each member has participated, the chairman will usually ask whether any member has any further questions, then will ask you if you have anything you wish to add. Unless you are expecting this question, it may floor you. Worse, it may start you off on an extended, extemporaneous speech. The board is not usually seeking more information. The question is principally to offer you a last opportunity to present further qualifications or to indicate that you have nothing to add. So, if you feel that a significant qualification or characteristic has been overlooked, it is proper to point it out in a sentence or so. Do not compliment the board on the thoroughness of their examination – they have been sketchy, and you know it. If you wish, merely say, "No thank you, I have nothing further to add." This is a point where you can "talk yourself out" of a good impression or fail to present an important bit of information. Remember, *you close the interview yourself.*

The chairman will then say, "That is all, Mr. _____, thank you." Do not be startled; the interview is over, and quicker than you think. Thank him, gather your belongings and take your leave. Save your sigh of relief for the other side of the door.

How to put your best foot forward

Throughout this entire process, you may feel that the board individually and collectively is trying to pierce your defenses, seek out your hidden weaknesses and embarrass and confuse you. Actually, this is not true. They are obliged to make an appraisal of your qualifications for the job you are seeking, and they want to see you in your best light. Remember, they must interview all candidates and a non-cooperative candidate may become a failure in spite of their best efforts to bring out his qualifications. Here are 15 suggestions that will help you:

1) Be natural – Keep your attitude confident, not cocky

If you are not confident that you can do the job, do not expect the board to be. Do not apologize for your weaknesses, try to bring out your strong points. The board is interested in a positive, not negative, presentation. Cockiness will antagonize any board member and make him wonder if you are covering up a weakness by a false show of strength.

2) Get comfortable, but don't lounge or sprawl

Sit erectly but not stiffly. A careless posture may lead the board to conclude that you are careless in other things, or at least that you are not impressed by the importance of the occasion. Either conclusion is natural, even if incorrect. Do not fuss with your clothing, a pencil or an ashtray. Your hands may occasionally be useful to emphasize a point; do not let them become a point of distraction.

3) Do not wisecrack or make small talk

This is a serious situation, and your attitude should show that you consider it as such. Further, the time of the board is limited – they do not want to waste it, and neither should you.

4) Do not exaggerate your experience or abilities

In the first place, from information in the application or other interviews and sources, the board may know more about you than you think. Secondly, you probably will not get away with it. An experienced board is rather adept at spotting such a situation, so do not take the chance.

5) If you know a board member, do not make a point of it, yet do not hide it

Certainly you are not fooling him, and probably not the other members of the board. Do not try to take advantage of your acquaintanceship – it will probably do you little good.

6) Do not dominate the interview

Let the board do that. They will give you the clues – do not assume that you have to do all the talking. Realize that the board has a number of questions to ask you, and do not try to take up all the interview time by showing off your extensive knowledge of the answer to the first one.

7) Be attentive

You only have 20 minutes or so, and you should keep your attention at its sharpest throughout. When a member is addressing a problem or question to you, give him your undivided attention. Address your reply principally to him, but do not exclude the other board members.

8) Do not interrupt

A board member may be stating a problem for you to analyze. He will ask you a question when the time comes. Let him state the problem, and wait for the question.

9) Make sure you understand the question

Do not try to answer until you are sure what the question is. If it is not clear, restate it in your own words or ask the board member to clarify it for you. However, do not haggle about minor elements.

10) Reply promptly but not hastily

A common entry on oral board rating sheets is "candidate responded readily," or "candidate hesitated in replies." Respond as promptly and quickly as you can, but do not jump to a hasty, ill-considered answer.

11) Do not be peremptory in your answers

A brief answer is proper – but do not fire your answer back. That is a losing game from your point of view. The board member can probably ask questions much faster than you can answer them.

12) Do not try to create the answer you think the board member wants

He is interested in what kind of mind you have and how it works – not in playing games. Furthermore, he can usually spot this practice and will actually grade you down on it.

13) Do not switch sides in your reply merely to agree with a board member

Frequently, a member will take a contrary position merely to draw you out and to see if you are willing and able to defend your point of view. Do not start a debate, yet do not surrender a good position. If a position is worth taking, it is worth defending.

14) Do not be afraid to admit an error in judgment if you are shown to be wrong

The board knows that you are forced to reply without any opportunity for careful consideration. Your answer may be demonstrably wrong. If so, admit it and get on with the interview.

15) Do not dwell at length on your present job

The opening question may relate to your present assignment. Answer the question but do not go into an extended discussion. You are being examined for a *new* job, not your present one. As a matter of fact, try to phrase ALL your answers in terms of the job for which you are being examined.

Basis of Rating

Probably you will forget most of these "do's" and "don'ts" when you walk into the oral interview room. Even remembering them all will not ensure you a passing grade. Perhaps you did not have the qualifications in the first place. But remembering them will help you to put your best foot forward, without treading on the toes of the board members.

Rumor and popular opinion to the contrary notwithstanding, an oral board wants you to make the best appearance possible. They know you are under pressure – but they also want to see how you respond to it as a guide to what your reaction would be under the pressures of the job you seek. They will be influenced by the degree of poise you display, the personal traits you show and the manner in which you respond.

ABOUT THIS BOOK

This book contains tests divided into Examination Sections. Go through each test, answering every question in the margin. We have also attached a sample answer sheet at the back of the book that can be removed and used. At the end of each test look at the answer key and check your answers. On the ones you got wrong, look at the right answer choice and learn. Do not fill in the answers first. Do not memorize the questions and answers, but understand the answer and principles involved. On your test, the questions will likely be different from the samples. Questions are changed and new ones added. If you understand these past questions you should have success with any changes that arise. Tests may consist of several types of questions. We have additional books on each subject should more study be advisable or necessary for you. Finally, the more you study, the better prepared you will be. This book is intended to be the last thing you study before you walk into the examination room. Prior study of relevant texts is also recommended. NLC publishes some of these in our Fundamental Series. Knowledge and good sense are important factors in passing your exam. Good luck also helps. So now study this Passbook, absorb the material contained within and take that knowledge into the examination. Then do your best to pass that exam.

EXAMINATION SECTION

EXAMINATION SECTION
TEST 1

DIRECTIONS: Each question or incomplete statement is followed by several suggested answers or completions. Select the one that BEST answers the question or completes the statement. *PRINT THE LETTER OF THE CORRECT ANSWER IN THE SPACE AT THE RIGHT.*

1. Of the following, the hazard MOST likely to damage rubber tubes in storage is

    A. breakage
    B. combustion
    C. corrosion
    D. deterioration

    1.____

2. Of the following, the hazard MOST likely to damage vacuum tubes in storage is

    A. breakage
    B. corrosion
    C. deterioration
    D. evaporation

    2.____

3. In checking large numbers of incoming supplies of a single item, the BEST practice to follow is to

    A. count the total number of containers received and only count the number of units in some of the containers
    B. count the total number of containers received only in those shipments where there is some doubt
    C. open all exterior containers received and count the number of containers inside when there are interior containers
    D. open all exterior and interior containers received and count the exact number of units

    3.____

4. Some experts advise that barrels containing liquids should be turned occasionally. The BEST reason for this is to

    A. enable a check of the condition of the barrel
    B. enable a check of the condition of the contents
    C. keep the contents well mixed
    D. prevent the wood from drying out

    4.____

5. For day-to-day protection when working in a room or enclosure containing combustible or explosive gases or gasolines, it would be MOST advisable to wear

    A. a general purpose gas mask
    B. a synthetic rubber suit
    C. non-sparking shoes
    D. rubber-framed goggles

    5.____

6. The one of the following which is NOT recommended as a method of reducing the possibility of spontaneous combustion of burlap bags is to

    A. air them out before stacking
    B. dampen them slightly before stacking
    C. keep them off concrete floors
    D. keep them away from brick walls

    6.____

7. When oxygen is leaking from a gas cylinder and the valve cannot close properly, the MOST advisable course of action to take while waiting for the valve to be repaired is to

   A. evacuate the building
   B. have it sent to a using agency before more oxygen is lost
   C. place the cylinder in the room with the poorest ventilation
   D. remove the cylinder from the building

8. Assume that you have to move four cartons to a location about 35 feet away. Each carton weighs 20 pounds and measures 2' x 8' x 4'.
   Of the following, the method of moving the cartons which would ordinarily be BEST is to

   A. have a team of two men make four trips
   B. have two teams of two men each carry two cartons
   C. make one trip using a four-wheel handtruck
   D. make one trip using a two-wheel handtruck

9. Assume that you have to move one carton to a location about 15 feet away. The carton weighs about 30 pounds and measures 8" x 18" x 24".
   Of the following, the method of moving the carton which would ordinarily be BEST is to

   A. have one man carry it
   B. have two men carry it
   C. put it on a two-wheel handtruck
   D. put it on a four-wheel handtruck

10. Assume that you have to move ten 45-pound cartons to a location about 75 feet away. Each carton measures 24" x 24" x 24".
    Of the following, the method of moving the cartons which would ordinarily be BEST is to

    A. load them on a pallet and use a forklift truck
    B. load them on a skid and push the skid
    C. load them on a trailer and pull it with a tractor
    D. use a portable conveyor

Questions 11-16.

DIRECTIONS: Questions 11 through 16 are to be answered SOLELY on the basis of the following table.

REPORT OF SEMI-ANNUAL INVENTORY

Article	Physical Inventory				Perpetual Inventory		Adjustment	
	Unit	Qty.	Price	Amt.	Qty.	Amt.	Qty.	Amt.
Batteries, flashlight	ea.	63	.08	5.04	60	14.80	+3	+.24
Bolts, flat head with square nuts, 100 in box	box	23	1.47	33.80	25	36.75		
Fuse, 15 amp, 4 in box	box	80	.07	5.60	80	5.60		
Fuse, 20 amp, 4 in box	box	77	.07	5.39	80	5.60	3	.21
Tape, friction, 50 ft. to a roll	roll	45	.22	9.90	45	9.90		
Washers, 100 in can 1/8" beveled	can	35	.32	11.20	35	11.20		
3/8" beveled	can	41	.33	13.53	45	14.85	4	1.32
Totals				84.47		88.70		

11. In the above report, for which item is there an INCORRECT entry? 11._____
    A. 15 amp. fuses B. Friction tape
    C. Flashlight batteries D. 1/8" washers

12. In the above report, adjustments were omitted for _____ article(s). 12._____
    A. one B. two C. three D. four

13. After all appropriate entries have been made in the Adjustment column, the total which must be deducted from the book value of the inventory is 13._____
    A. $1.53 B. $1.77 C. $4.23 D. $4.71

14. The quantities shown in Perpetual Inventory exceed those shown in Physical Inventory by a total of 14._____
    A. 4 B. 6 C. 10 D. 12

15. The cost of ten washers, 1/8" beveled, is MOST NEARLY 15._____
    A. $.003 B. $.032 C. $.320 D. $3.20

16. The cost of 24 fuses is MOST NEARLY 16._____
    A. $.28 B. $.42 C. $.80 D. $1.68

17. Assume that you are in charge of a group of four men who are to carry an oak beam measuring 8" x 8" x 18' from one point to another.
    Of the following, the BEST method of carrying the beam is to have

    A. the men arrange themselves at equal distances along one side of the beam and carry the beam at their sides
    B. the men arrange themselves at equal distances on opposite sides of the beam and carry the beam at waist height
    C. the men arrange themselves in order of height along the beam so that the beam may be carried on the shoulders of all of the men
    D. two men stand at one end of the beam and two men at the other end in order to lift the beam on to the shoulders of the two strongest men

18. Although the old model of a certain item has been replaced by a new model which is interchangeable with the old model, most requisitions call specifically for the old model. Since your stock of the old model is almost depleted, it would be MOST advisable for you to

    A. establish a carefully regulated system of priorities based on need
    B. inform the source of your supply of the continued demand for the old model
    C. inform the using agencies or individuals of the feasibility of substituting the new model
    D. substitute the new model whenever the old model is called for

19. An assistant stockman is assigned by you to take physical inventory of a particular small part stored in several open boxes. This part is of uniform size and is packaged 100 to a box. He returns in an unusually short time with the count. His explanation for his speed is that he consolidated all the items as much as possible so that all except one box were full. He multiplied 100 by the number of boxes and added the number of additional parts left.
    Of the following, the MOST advisable course of action for you to take is to

    A. compliment him on his efficiency
    B. explain the proper way of taking inventory
    C. have him watch a more experienced worker take inventory
    D. suggest that he ask permission before changing procedure

20. In determining the number of months of supply to be ordered at one time, the LEAST important of the following factors is the

    A. average market price
    B. deterioration rate
    C. discount for quantity
    D. money available for purchasing

21. A check during physical inventory has revealed that many of the bottles of alcohol do not contain sixteen ounces as indicated on the labels.
    Of the following, the MOST advisable action to take FIRST is to

    A. check future shipments by the vendor immediately upon their arrival
    B. see if the bottles are tightly capped
    C. see if the cartons are wet
    D. question your subordinates about the situation

22. Of the following, the FIRST thing which should be done in order to determine the reason for a discrepancy between the perpetual inventory card and the bin card or other similar record is to

    A. check the original requisitions
    B. compare each transaction listed on both cards
    C. ascertain whether any stock has been transferred to another warehouse
    D. question all personnel involved

    22._____

23. Items such as tools are sometimes issued on a temporary basis and are to be returned after use so that they may be issued again when needed. In such cases, a record of each withdrawal

    A. need not be kept
    B. should be made on an inventory card
    C. should be made on a locator card
    D. should be made on a separate register

    23._____

24. Assume that you have 100 boxes of a particular item on hand. Since this is the minimum order point, you have already ordered 300 boxes, which is the usual 6 months' supply. This order has not yet been delivered, and you have just received a requisition for 1,000 boxes.
    Of the following, the MOST advisable action for you to take FIRST is to

    A. order an additional 1,000 boxes
    B. order an additional 1,300 boxes
    C. ascertain the reason for such a requisition
    D. inform the ordering agency that the requisition cannot be filled immediately

    24._____

Questions 25-27.

DIRECTIONS: Questions 25 through 27 are based on the following method of obtaining a reorder point: multiply the monthly rate of consumption by the lead time (in months) and add the minimum balance.

25. If the reorder point is 250 units, the lead time is 2 months, and the average monthly rate of consumption is 75 units, then the minimum balance is _____ units.

    A. 75   B. 100   C. 150   D. 250

    25._____

26. If the lead time is 30 days, the minimum balance is 200 units, and the average monthly rate of consumption is 100 units, then the reorder point is _____ units.

    A. 100   B. 200   C. 300   D. 400

    26._____

27. If the reorder point is 300 units, the lead time is 2 months, and the minimum balance is 100 units, then the average monthly rate of consumption is _____ units.

    A. 50   B. 100   C. 200   D. 300

    27._____

28. You are planning to submit an initial order for a new item. You estimate that you will issue 100 per month, and you want to have a two-month supply in reserve. You will reorder this item every six months. Your initial order should be for

    A. 200   B. 600   C. 700   D. 800

    28._____

29. For a particular item, the reorder point is established at 585. If the average rate of consumption is 130 and the lead time is 3 months, then the amount which should be on hand when the new delivery is received is

    A. 130 B. 195 C. 260 D. 325

30. You have room in the storehouse for 750 cartons of a certain item. Assume that you issue 125 cartons per month and keep a one-month supply in reserve. Delivery time is thirty days.
    Which of the following would it be MOST appropriate to order under these conditions?
    _____ every _____ months.

    A. 250; 3 B. 500; 3 C. 375; 4 D. 500; 4

31. Using maximum loads when transporting stock is

    A. *desirable* because it results in fewer trips
    B. *desirable* because it simplifies accounting and clerical work
    C. *undesirable* because it shortens the life of the equipment
    D. *undesirable* because it strains the capacity of the workers

32. Of the following, the BEST single basis for determining the desirability of purchasing new stock-handling equipment is the

    A. ability of the workers to handle the equipment
    B. condition of the present equipment
    C. estimated savings in costs
    D. size of the warehouse or stock facility

33. Frequent rest periods are MOST desirable when

    A. the men have been doing a good job
    B. the morale of the men is low
    C. there is a great deal of heavy work
    D. there is not too much work

34. In terms of plant economy, a storehouse is operating at GREATEST efficiency when it stores _____ stock that it is designed to hold.

    A. 10% less B. 10% more
    C. 50% more D. the exact amount of

35. Of the following, the one which a foreman or supervisor can MOST readily increase or improve is an employee's ability to

    A. get along with his fellow workers
    B. perform technical aspects of his job
    C. supervise others
    D. use good judgment in unusual situations

36. On one day, a certain piece of stock-handling equipment is not used at all. On the next day, several men are waiting to use it.
    This situation can BEST be corrected by

    A. having the men do the work manually
    B. keeping additional equipment available

C. posting a schedule for the use of the equipment
D. rearranging the work of the men

37. Despite all your efforts to streamline the work and make it more efficient, there still seems to be more work than you and your men can handle in a normal work week.
The MOST advisable course of action for you to take FIRST is to

   A. discuss the matter with your supervisor
   B. request more mechanical equipment
   C. request permission for overtime work
   D. tell your men that everyone will have to work a little harder

37.____

38. Assume that a subordinate tells you that he has made a mistake in filling out certain records.
The MOST advisable action for you to take FIRST is to

   A. explain how the job should have been done
   B. get another subordinate to do the job correctly
   C. tell him how to correct his mistake
   D. tell him to forget it but to do it correctly next time

38.____

39. Your supervisor gives you instructions which you feel are contrary to good storage procedure.
The MOST advisable action for you to take FIRST is to

   A. attempt to get additional support for your point of view
   B. follow his instructions without question
   C. suggest your method of doing the work
   D. say nothing but do the job the way you feel it should be done

39.____

40. You have reason to believe that one of your men is taking home merchandise from the storehouse. You question the man about this. He shows you that it was obsolete material of no value which was not salvageable and was about to be discarded.
Under these circumstances, the MOST appropriate action for you to take is to

   A. have him return the merchandise
   B. report the matter to your supervisor
   C. say nothing further
   D. tell the man that he should have asked your permission

40.____

41. Three new men have just been assigned to work under your supervision. Every time you give them an assignment, one of these men asks you several questions.
Of the following, the MOST advisable action for you to take is to

   A. assure him of your confidence in his ability to carry out the assignment correctly without asking so many questions
   B. have all three men listen to your answers to these questions
   C. point out that the other two men do the job without asking so many questions
   D. tell him to see if he can get the answers from other workers before coming to you

41.____

42. One of the men in your crew has continually been making derogatory statements about the personal life of one of the other men.
Of the following, it would probably be MOST advisable for you to

   A. attempt to obtain a transfer for the man who is the subject of the derogatory statements
   B. ignore the matter unless it has any effect on the work
   C. point out to your crew some of the weak spots in the character of the man who is making derogatory statements
   D. tell the man to stop making derogatory statements

43. Two of your subordinates suggest that you recommend a third man for an above-standard service rating because of his superior work.
You should

   A. ask the two subordinates whether the third man knows that they intended to discuss this matter with you
   B. explain to the two subordinates that an above-standard service rating for one man would have a detrimental effect on many of the other men
   C. recommend the man for an above-standard service rating if there is sufficient justification for it
   D. tell the two subordinates that the matter of service ratings is not their concern

44. At a meeting with your subordinates, which you have called in order to determine the best ways of dealing with some departmental policies, some of the men interrupt with comments and suggestions.
Of the following, the MOST advisable course of action for you to take in MOST cases is to

   A. encourage full but orderly participation by all the men
   B. end the meeting and issue a bulletin instead
   C. tell them to hold their comments and questions until after you have finished
   D. tell those who interrupt that they are being unfair to the others

45. When one of your subordinates takes unusually long lunch hours, you tell him that this practice must stop.
Of the following, the BEST reason for speaking to him about this is that

   A. he will take even longer lunch hours unless you speak to him
   B. morale of your other subordinates may be impaired unless the situation is corrected
   C. work cannot be done in time unless the practice is discontinued
   D. your other subordinates will take the same amount of time for lunch as he does

46. You have just been assigned a new employee who has had a college education but has had no experience in stock work. Of the following, the BEST course of action for you to take is to

   A. attempt to have him transferred as soon as possible
   B. explain to him that he probably would not like the work
   C. make special efforts to ease his relationships with the other workers
   D. treat him the same as you would treat any other new worker

47. The morale of your subordinates seems unusually high. They tell you that it is because they have heard that one of them is to get a provisional promotion. You know definitely that this is not true.
The MOST advisable action for you to take is to

   A. act as if you are happy to hear the good news
   B. let the situation take its normal course
   C. report the matter to your supervisor
   D. tell them that, so far as you know, the rumor is not justified

48. In most cases, the FIRST step to take in the event of serious injury in the storeroom is to

   A. search the employee for instructions pertaining to medical care
   B. send for medical help
   C. take the employee to a hospital
   D. treat the injury

49. An employee has accidentally cut his arm and is bleeding profusely.
The one of the following which should NOT be done is to

   A. apply pressure above the injury
   B. give the employee a mild stimulant
   C. keep the employee at complete rest
   D. raise the bleeding part

50. When gasoline and all other highly inflammable substances are stored outdoors, the *No Smoking* rule should be

   A. observed for indoor and outdoor storage areas
   B. observed for indoor storage areas only
   C. observed for outdoor storage areas only
   D. eliminated for indoor and outdoor storage areas

KEY (CORRECT ANSWERS)

1. D	11. C	21. B	31. A	41. B
2. A	12. A	22. B	32. C	42. D
3. A	13. C	23. D	33. C	43. C
4. D	14. B	24. C	34. D	44. A
5. C	15. B	25. B	35. B	45. B
6. B	16. B	26. C	36. D	46. D
7. D	17. A	27. B	37. A	47. D
8. C	18. C	28. D	38. C	48. B
9. A	19. A	29. B	39. C	49. B
10. A	20. A	30. D	40. D	50. A

EXAMINATION SECTION
TEST 1

DIRECTIONS: Each question or incomplete statement is followed by several suggested answers or completions. Select the one that BEST answers the question or completes the statement. *PRINT THE LETTER OF THE CORRECT ANSWER IN THE SPACE AT THE RIGHT.*

1. For the GREATEST economy in transporting stock, one should

    A. divide the load into as many easily managed units as possible
    B. replace machines with men whenever possible
    C. transport as large a load as possible at one time
    D. utilize conveyor belts for most transporting

    1.____

2. Assume that a new piece of equipment has been devised that would cut the labor cost of a certain major operation 75% and the time 50%. The monetary savings to the city would be such that the machine would pay for itself in one year. However, the old equipment is still in good working condition.
The MOST advisable recommendation to make is that the

    A. *new* equipment be purchased
    B. *new* equipment be purchased only if the old equipment can be sold at a reasonable price
    C. *new* equipment be rented
    D. *old* equipment be retained until there is moderate deterioration

    2.____

3. Economy in handling stock can be measured BEST in terms of the

    A. cost of the equipment used
    B. cost of stock-handling operations
    C. overhead cost plus depreciation of equipment
    D. salaries being paid to the men

    3.____

4. It is MOST economical and efficient to have good lighting available in

    A. all parts of the storehouse
    B. packing areas only
    C. receiving areas only
    D. storage areas only

    4.____

5. If a great deal of heavy work must be completed by men under your supervision, it is MOST advisable, when possible, to

    A. give frequent rest periods
    B. have the men work overtime
    C. have the men listen to lively music while working
    D. shorten the lunch hour

    5.____

6. A storehouse USUALLY operates at GREATEST efficiency when it stores _____ stock than it is designed to hold.

    A. slightly less   B. slightly more
    C. substantially more   D. the exact amount of

    6.____

7. Usually, a report should be prepared with AT LEAST

   A. one copy so that there is a copy for future reference
   B. two copies so that the report can be sent to more than one person
   C. two copies so that there is an extra copy for your supervisor
   D. three copies so that there will be sufficient copies if they are needed

8. Of the following, the one which can MOST easily be increased or improved in an employee by his foreman or supervisor is

   A. ability to learn   B. aptitude
   C. common sense   D. knowledge

9. Two men under your supervision who are required to work together are not able to get along with each other. You have attempted to remedy this situation but without any success. One is an older man who has been in the section for many years, and the other is a recently-appointed younger man. Both men are capable employees.
   Of the following, the MOST advisable course of action for you to take is to recommend that the

   A. older man be transferred
   B. two men be given below-average service ratings
   C. younger man be discharged at the end of his probationary period
   D. younger man be transferred

10. Inefficient scheduling of work should be suspected when one notes that there are several men

    A. absent from work   B. in the rest room
    C. loading a truck   D. waiting to use equipment

11. *It is better to haul than to carry.*
    The PRIMARY reason for this statement is that

    A. stock should not be placed on top of any movable equipment
    B. stockmen should not be allowed to carry stock for any great distance
    C. the same power can usually pull more than it can carry
    D. there is less danger of damage when stock is hauled

12. After you have given a newly-appointed subordinate complete instructions on how to use a handtruck, you should usually

    A. assign him to work with another subordinate
    B. go over the instructions once more
    C. let him use the handtruck while you watch him
    D. tell him about the importance of the work

13. One of your subordinates tells you that he wants to submit a suggestion to the suggestion program regarding the operation of the storeroom but that he wants your advice first. The MOST advisable course of action for you to take is to

    A. advise him that any suggestions concerning the storeroom should be made directly to you
    B. give him advice provided he includes your name on the suggestion

C. give him the advice he needs
D. tell him that it would not be fair if you were to give him any help

14. Assume that you are in charge of one section of a storehouse. When the man in charge of an adjoining section resigns, you are asked to assume that job in addition to your own. After several weeks, you find that it is impossible for you to provide adequate supervision for both sections.
Of the following, the BEST course of action for you to take is to

    A. ask your supervisor for a transfer
    B. assign one subordinate in each section the job of supervision
    C. divide your time between the two sections
    D. inform your supervisor of the facts

15. Your subordinates tell you that, in your absence, your supervisor gave them orders which differed from those which you had given them.
In this case, you should

    A. discuss the matter with your subordinates to determine which orders are correct
    B. discuss the matter with your supervisor
    C. tell your subordinates to follow your orders
    D. tell your subordinates to follow your supervisor's orders

16. Assume that one of your subordinates made an error in recording an issue of stock. The mistake was found and corrected, but your subordinate seems rather depressed about the matter.
Of the following, the MOST advisable course of action for you to take is to

    A. ignore the entire situation unless it happens again
    B. praise him
    C. reprimand him mildly
    D. show him how he can avoid such a mistake in the future

17. Assume that you have the following equipment available: two forklift trucks, one tractor, six trailers, and four handtrucks.
In order to move twenty pallet loads 200 yards in a storehouse, it would be MOST advisable for you to use the

    A. forklift trucks
    B. forklift trucks, the tractor, and the trailers
    C. handtrucks, the tractor, and the trailers
    D. tractor and the trailers

18. Small cartons to be stored for a period of a year would usually be BEST stored on

    A. dollies   B. pallets   C. the floor   D. trailers

19. The one of the following types of equipment which should generally be used to collect a small number of items from various parts of the storehouse for a single shipment is a

    A. four-wheel truck   B. pallet
    C. skid   D. two-wheel truck

20. In a large city storehouse, main aisles used for movement of materials should usually be NOT less than _____ ft.

    A. 1　　　B. 2　　　C. 4　　　D. 6

21. An aisle used only as a fire aisle should be APPROXIMATELY _____ feet wide.

    A. 2　　　B. 5　　　C. 8　　　D. 10

22. When a perishable commodity is received at the storeroom, the factor which is generally LEAST important to consider when deciding where to store it is the

    A. activity of the commodity
    B. size and weight of the commodity
    C. temperature and humidity of the storage areas
    D. total storage capacity of the storeroom

23. Ten cartons of a certain item are stacked on each of ten pallets standing in a row. Assume that the men and equipment mentioned below are available.
    In order to move the cartons, with or without the pallets, from their place in the storehouse into a waiting truck, a distance of 25 yards, it would be MOST efficient to

    A. form a line of men to pass the cartons into the truck
    B. have a forklift truck take each pallet load separately and load it on the truck
    C. have one man move each pallet load with a hand lift pallet truck
    D. transfer the cartons from the pallets to a single tractor trailer train and then load them on the truck

24. The one of the following circumstances in which it would be MOST appropriate to use a fixed-platform power truck rather than a forklift truck is when

    A. loading a railroad car
    B. miscellaneous small items must be selected for a single shipment
    C. the load must be carried over a long distance
    D. there is a shortage of manpower

25. Storing small items in their original containers is a

    A. *bad* practice because it encourages laziness
    B. *bad* practice because it is disorderly
    C. *good* practice because it decreases handling
    D. *good* practice because it eliminates the need for shelves and bins

KEY (CORRECT ANSWERS)

1.	C	11.	C
2.	A	12.	C
3.	B	13.	C
4.	A	14.	D
5.	A	15.	B
6.	D	16.	D
7.	A	17.	B
8.	D	18.	B
9.	D	19.	A
10.	D	20.	D

21. A
22. D
23. B
24. B
25. C

TEST 2

DIRECTIONS: Each question or incomplete statement is followed by several suggested answers or completions. Select the one that BEST answers the question or completes the statement. *PRINT THE LETTER OF THE CORRECT ANSWER IN THE SPACE AT THE RIGHT.*

1. Assume that you have to move two cartons to a location about 50 feet away. Each carton weighs 10 pounds and measures 2' x 4' x 4'.
   Of the following, the method of moving the cartons which would ordinarily be BEST is to

   A. have two men carry each carton
   B. make one trip using a two-wheel handtruck
   C. make two trips using a two-wheel handtruck
   D. put both cartons on a four-wheel handtruck

   1.____

2. Assume that you have to move two cartons to a location about 25 feet away. Each carton weighs 10 pounds and measures 6" x 12" x 18".
   Of the following, the method of moving the cartons which would ordinarily be BEST is to

   A. have one man carry both cartons in one trip
   B. have one man make two trips
   C. put both cartons on a four-wheel handtruck
   D. put both cartons on a two-wheel handtruck

   2.____

3. Assume that you have to move twenty 10-pound cartons to a location about 100 feet away.
   Of the following, the method of moving the cartons which would ordinarily be BEST is to

   A. get a team of men to carry them by hand
   B. load them on a pallet and use a forklift truck
   C. load them on a skid and push the skid
   D. make a line of men and pass them from hand to hand

   3.____

4. Assume that you have to move fifty pallets from one location in the warehouse to another about 250 feet away. Of the following, the equipment that you would need to do the job MOST efficiently is

   A. forklift truck, tractor, trailers
   B. four-wheel handtruck, portable elevator
   C. two-wheel handtruck, tractor, trailers
   D. two-wheel handtruck, trailers

   4.____

5. The principle of *first-in, first-out* should generally be applied

   A. only to commodities subject to deterioration
   B. only to dated commodities
   C. only to perishable commodities
   D. to most commodities

   5.____

6. A worker who is lifting a heavy object from the floor to a shoulder height position should preferably

   A. bend his knees, keep his back straight, and jerk the object to shoulder height in one quick motion
   B. bend his knees, keep his back straight, and lift to shoulder height in a slow continuous motion
   C. lift the object waist high, rest one end of it on a ledge, and then, while bending the knees, raise it to shoulder height
   D. lift the object waist high, rest one end of it on a ledge, and then, while keeping the knees straight, raise it to shoulder height

7. You have in stock a full drum of liquid which is lying on its side. You assign two men to stand it upright.
   The proper position for the men to take is for _____ to stand _____ of the drum.

   A. both; at the bottom end
   B. both; at the top end
   C. each; on opposite ends
   D. each; on opposite sides

8. Assume that you are employed in a well organized storehouse. Your stock records indicate that 450 units of a certain commodity are in stock. You count these items on a shelf and find only 175.
   The MOST advisable action for you to take FIRST is to

   A. consult the locator system
   B. count these items again
   C. recompute the stock balance
   D. report the shortage

9. A certain item is stored in a number of locations throughout a storeroom. You have counted the items in each location and added the numbers to get the total.
   Of the following, the BEST way to make sure that your figures are correct is to

   A. add the numbers again, using a different method
   B. add the numbers again, using the same method
   C. count the items again and recompute
   D. move all the items to one location

10. In taking inventory, you count much more of a certain iten than is shown on the inventory card.
    Of the following, the MOST advisable action for you to take FIRST is to

    A. put an adjusting entry on the inventory card
    B. refer the matter to your supervisor
    C. review all requisitions since the last inventory record
    D. recheck the figures on the card

11. Assume that paper is issued at the rate of 500 reams per month. Three-hole punches are issued at the rate of 1 a month.
    Of the following alternatives, it would probably be MOST practical and economic to order

    A. 500 reams per month and one three-hole punch per month
    B. 1,500 reams four times a year and 12 three-hole punches once a year
    C. 2,000 reams three times a year and 60 three-hole punches once every 5 years
    D. 18,000 reams once every 3 years and 36 three-hole punches once every 3 years

12. Assume that the price of an item is much lower during the months of June, July, and August However, you issue it throughout the year at the rate of 100 per month. The delivery time is one month, and you keep a one-month's reserve on hand at all times. You have enough room for 600 items.
    Of the following, it would ordinarily be BEST for you to order

    A. 200 in June, 500 in August, and 500 in January
    B. 400 in June, 400 in August, and 400 in December
    C. 600 in July and 600 in December
    D. 500 in June, 200 in July, and 500 in August

13. Assume that one of the items which you stock is issued only during April, May, and June at the rate of 400 per month. You keep a one-month's supply on hand at all times, although you have sufficient room for an unlimited supply. The delivery time is one month.
    Assuming that there are sufficient funds available at all times, it would probably be BEST for you to order

    A. 100 each month of the year
    B. 400 in March, 400 in April, and 400 in May
    C. 400 in April, 400 in May, and 400 in June
    D. 1,200 in March

14. Assume that you stock an item which deteriorates rapidly after 2 months. This item is issued at an average rate of 100 per month. The delivery time is one month. You keep a reserve supply of 20.
    If these figures are maintained, you should order _____ iteris once _____ month(s).

    A. 100; a   B. 200; every two
    C. 220; every two   D. 300; every three

15. Assume that you have 50 boxes of a particular item on hand. The minimum order point is 100, and you have already ordered 300 boxes, which is the usual 3-months' supply. This order has not yet been delivered, and you have just received a special requisition for an additional 300 boxes.
    Of the following, the MOST advisable action for you to take is to order

    A. 300 boxes immediately
    B. 300 boxes as soon as your outstanding order has been received
    C. 600 boxes immediately
    D. 600 boxes at the end of the present 3-month period

16. When a new model of a certain item is manufactured, you still have in stock a number of items of the old model. The old model is usable, but all the requisitions call for the new model.
Asking the requesting agencies or individuals to accept the old model instead is

   A. *desirable* because the best items should be issued last
   B. *desirable* because you will not be left with obsolete stock
   C. *undesirable* because it is interfering with their prerogatives
   D. *undesirable* because they should not be penalized for your errors

17. You are planning to submit an initial order for a new item. You estimate that you will issue 10 per month, and you want to have a one month's supply in reserve. You will reorder this item every three months.
Your initial order should be for

   A. 10   B. 20   C. 30   D. 40

18. You have room in the storehouse for 1,000 cartons of a certain item. Assume that you issue 100 boxes per month and always keep a one-month's supply in reserve. You order supplies every six months. Delivery time is thirty days.
Of the following, the MOST appropriate amount to order under usual circumstances is

   A. 500   B. 600   C. 700   D. 1,000

19. The PRINCIPAL disadvantage of having an order-picker fill two or more orders at one time is that

   A. more equipment is needed
   B. the order-picker will resent the burden
   C. the work must be scheduled more precisely
   D. there is greater chance of error

20. Of the following, the MOST important reason for having a physical inventory as well as a perpetual inventory is that a physical inventory

   A. enables a physical inspection of the items to determine their condition
   B. familiarizes the men with the stock
   C. gives a count of the number of items actually on hand
   D. provides an opportunity to clean up the area

21. Of the following conditions, the one which is properly represented by an annual stock turnover of 2.0 is _____ original stock has been replaced _____.

   A. half of the; during the year
   B. the; once during the year
   C. the; twice during the year
   D. the; once every two months

22. Of the following kinds of items, the one for which frequent inspections are MOST necessary is the item which is

   A. dated   B. heavy   C. plastic   D. small

23. Of the following items, the one for which physical counts should be made MOST frequently is

    A. nails   B. pipes   C. valves   D. wrenches

24. In order to avoid any interruption in normal storehouse operations during physical inventory, it would be necessary to

    A. close each section as it is inventoried
    B. close the storehouse during inventory
    C. inventory only on alternate days
    D. inventory after working hours or on weekends

25. It would be desirable to reduce stock levels to a one month period when the item is

    A. *expensive* and can be readily obtained
    B. *expensive* and difficult to obtain
    C. *inexpensive* and can be readily obtained
    D. *inexpensive* and difficult to obtain

KEY (CORRECT ANSWERS)

1.	D	11.	B
2.	A	12.	B
3.	B	13.	D
4.	A	14.	A
5.	D	15.	A
6.	C	16.	B
7.	D	17.	D
8.	A	18.	B
9.	C	19.	D
10.	D	20.	C

21. C
22. A
23. D
24. D
25. A

EXAMINATION SECTION
TEST 1

DIRECTIONS: Each question or incomplete statement is followed by several suggested answers or completions. Select the one that BEST answers the question or completes the statement. *PRINT THE LETTER OF THE CORRECT ANSWER IN THE SPACE AT THE RIGHT.*

1. One of the results of understocking is that

   A. more money is tied up in stock
   B. stock must be ordered more frequently
   C. there is greater likelihood of obsolescence
   D. there is uneven distribution of materials in storage

   1._____

2. Assume that your re-order point is obtained by multiplying the monthly rate of consumption by the lead time (in months) and adding the minimum balance. For a particular item, the re-order point is established at 200 units.
   If the lead time is 2 months and the minimum balance is 100, then the average monthly rate of consumption is

   A. 50   B. 100   C. 150   D. 200

   2._____

3. If a certain item has shown no activity for two years, the MOST advisable action to take FIRST is to

   A. attempt to dispose of the item through salvage
   B. contact the using agencies or individuals to determine whether they can use the item
   C. contact the vendor to determine whether the item can be traded in
   D. write it off on the inventory control card

   3._____

4. The MOST important information on an inventory control card is that which gives the _____ of the item.

   A. identity   B. location
   C. rate of consumption   D. vendor

   4._____

5. A space 5 1/4 feet wide and 2 1/3 feet long has an area measuring MOST NEARLY _____ square feet.

   A. 9   B. 10   C. 11   D. 12

   5._____

6. One man is able to load two 2 1/2-ton trucks in one hour. To load ten such trucks, it will take ten men _____ hour(s).

   A. 1/2   B. 1   C. 2   D. 2 1/2

   6._____

7. If the average height of the stacks in your section of the storehouse is 10 feet, the area which will be occupied by 56,000 cubic feet of supplies is MOST likely to be

   A. 70' x 80'   B. 60' x 90'   C. 50' x 60'   D. 560' x 100'

   7._____

8. The number of cartons, each measuring two cubic feet, which can fit into a space which is 100 square feet in area and is 8 feet high is MOST NEARLY

   A. 50   B. 200   C. 400   D. 800

9. When the floor area measures 200 feet by 200 feet and the maximum weight it can hold is 4,000 tons, then the safe floor load is _____ pounds per square foot.

   A. 20   B. 160   C. 200   D. 400

10. A carton 1' x 1' x 3' measures _____ cubic yards.

    A. 1/3   B. 1/9   C. 3   D. 9

11. You have received six cartons, each containing sixty boxes of staples, priced at $36.00 per carton.
    The price per box is

    A. $.10   B. $.60   C. $3.60   D. $6.00

12. The amount of space, in cubic feet, required to store 100 boxes each measuring 24" x 12" x 6" is MOST NEARLY

    A. 10   B. 100   C. 168   D. 1008

13. Assume that it takes an average of two man-hours to stack 1 ton of certain supplies. In order to stack 30 tons, the number of men required to complete the job in ten hours is

    A. 6   B. 10   C. 15   D. 30

14. An area measures 20 feet by 22 1/2 feet. The floor load is 100 pounds per square foot. The total weight that can be stored in this area is MOST NEARLY _____ pounds.

    A. 450   B. 9,000   C. 22,500   D. 45,000

15. The price of a certain type of linoleum is $.20 per square foot.
    The total cost of four pieces of 9' x 12' linoleum is MOST NEARLY

    A. $21   B. $80   C. $86   D. $432

16. The number of board feet in a piece of lumber measuring 2 inches thick by 2 feet wide by 12 feet long is

    A. 12   B. 16   C. 24   D. 48

17. If 39 3/8 ounces of a certain commodity are on hand and two requisitions are filled, one for 9 1/2 and one for 9 5/6 ounces, the number of ounces remaining are

    A. 18 2/3   B. 19 1/3   C. 20 1/24   D. 20 3/4

18. In order to fill 96 bottles containing 3 fluid ounces each, the number of pints which would be needed is

    A. 9   B. 18   C. 32   D. 36

19. If a section of a storeroom measures 29 feet 4 inches by 18 feet 3 inches, the total area is MOST NEARLY _____ square feet.

    A. 523   B. 524   C. 535   D. 537

20. A discount of 1% is given on all purchases of over 100 brushes. An additional discount of 1% is given on all purchases of over 500 brushes.
If 600 brushes are purchased at a list price of $2.07 each, the total cost is MOST NEARLY

    A. $1217   B. $1228   C. $1230   D. $2484

21. The following items are purchased: 30 locksets at $15.00 per dozen, and 10 gross of stove bolts at 1 1/2 cents each bolt.
The total cost is MOST NEARLY

    A. $60   B. $180   C. $255   D. $470

22. The cost of one dozen pieces of screening, each measuring 4'6" by 5', at $.10 per square foot, is

    A. $22.50   B. $25.00   C. $27.00   D. $27.60

23. The amount of turpentine on hand is 39 gallons. One requisition is filled for 3 1/2 gallons, three additional requisitions are filled for 3 quarts each, and six requisitions are filled for 1 pint each.
The quantity of turpentine remaining after all these requisitions have been filled is

    A. 32 gal.   B. 32 gal. 1 qt.
    C. 32 gal. 2 qts.   D. 32 gal. 3 qts.

24. A shelf is 30" wide and 20" deep. The shelf is filled solid with 500 boxes, each measuring 2" x 3" x 5". The distance from the shelf to the top of the stacked boxes is

    A. 10"   B. 25"   C. 50"   D. 60"

25. In order to check on a shipment of 1000 articles, a sampling of 100 articles was carefully inspected.
Of the sample, one article was wholly defective and 4 more were partly defective.
On this basis, the percentage of completely acceptable articles in the original shipment is probably MOST NEARLY

    A. 5%   B. 10%   C. 95%   D. 100%

26. The one of the following which is NOT the name of a type of screwdriver is

    A. cabinet   B. flat-nose
    C. knife handle   D. spiral ratchet

27. Pupil Dental Record forms are likely to be used in GREATEST quantities by the

    A. Board of Education   B. Department of Health
    C. Department of Hospitals   D. Department of Social Service

28. Crepe paper is likely to be requisitioned MOST frequently by the

    A. Board of Education   B. Department of Public Events
    C. Housing Authority   D. Transit Authority

29. Scalpels are likely to be requisitioned MOST frequently by the Department of

    A. Correction   B. Health
    C. Hospitals   D. Parks

30. Pruners are likely to be requisitioned MOST frequently by the

    A. Department of Parks   B. Department of Sanitation
    C. Reference Library   D. Transit Authority

31. Fustats are likely to be requisitioned MOST frequently by the

    A. Department of Markets   B. Fire Department
    C. Housing Authority   D. Police Department

32. Machine screws are usually purchased in large quantities by the

    A. bushel   B. gross   C. pound   D. score

33. A No. 10 can of fruit juice contains about

    A. eight ounces   B. one pint
    C. one quart   D. three quarts

34. Sulphuric acid is USUALLY purchased in large quantities by the

    A. carboy   B. drum   C. gallon   D. cylinder

35. The one of the following which is NOT a standard size of index card is

    A. 3x5   B. 4x6   C. 5 x 7   D. 5 x 8

36. The label on a package of mimeograph paper reads: Size 8 1/2 x 11, Basis 20. *Basis 20* refers to the

    A. color code for this type of paper
    B. quality and finish of the paper
    C. way in which the paper is packaged
    D. weight of the paper

37. You tell a man to separate and store cans of paint in a certain way. The man then asks you, *Why do you want me to do it this way?*
    You should answer his question by

    A. advising him to figure out the reason himself
    B. explaining to him why you want it done in that particular way
    C. repeating your instructions more slowly
    D. telling him to follow your instructions without asking any questions

38. Assume that an employee shows you that you have made an error in issuing certain instructions. You admit your error.
    Such action on your part is desirable PRIMARILY because

    A. the job may be done correctly
    B. your men will be encouraged to make similar corrections in the future
    C. you will gain a reputation for fairness
    D. your men will realize that you will not make errors of this type in the future

39. Assume that you have just been promoted. Your supervisor gives you detailed oral instructions as to how a particular category of stock should be stored. At the conclusion of his instructions, you realize that you do not fully understand how your supervisor wishes to have the stock stored.
Under these circumstances, you should

    A. ask an experienced worker to clarify your supervisor's instructions
    B. ask your supervisor to clarify anything that you do not understand
    C. ask your supervisor to put his instructions in writing
    D. carry out your supervisor's instructions as best as you can

39.____

40. You have reason to believe that one of your men is taking merchandise which does not belong to him from the storehouse. You question the man about this. He tells you that he borrowed the merchandise and intends to return it. Under these Circumstances, you should probably

    A. disregard the matter until such time as you have evidence which will stand up in court
    B. offer to accompany the man to his home to pick up the property in question
    C. report the matter to your supervisor
    D. tell the man to return the property as soon as he has finished using it

40.____

41. A truck which must be unloaded immediately arrives at the storehouse. You issue instructions to your crew as to how this should be done. One of your men strongly objects and says that your instructions are wrong. You listen to his reasons but you still think that you are right. Under these circumstances, you should

    A. ask for opinions from the other men in the crew as to how the job should be done
    B. contact another worker to get his opinion
    C. refer the matter to your supervisor for his decision
    D. tell the men to unload the truck in accordance with your instructions

41.____

42. Whenever you give an assignment to one of your experienced men, he asks you a great many questions about it although he has successfully performed similar assignments in the past. The time you spend in answering his many questions about minor details takes you away from more important work.
Under these circumstances, you should probably FIRST

    A. answer his questions in such a way that he will be discouraged from asking further questions
    B. ask the man to ask his questions of one of his fellow employees
    C. assure the man of your confidence in his ability to carry out the assignment
    D. tell the man that if the assignment is too difficult you will give it to someone who does not raise so many questions

42.____

43. You have reason to believe that one of the men in your crew gossips about you behind your back.
Under these circumstances, it is usually BEST to

    A. attempt to find out which of your men believes the gossip
    B. find out what the man's weak points are and bring them to the attention of your crew

43.____

C. ignore the matter
D. speak to the man about it and tell him to stop

44. Your supervisor gives you an assignment which you believe you cannot do since you do not have a sufficient number of men. You explain this to your supervisor but he tells you to get the job done.
You should

   A. do the best you can and keep your supervisor informed of the progress you are making
   B. report the matter to your main office
   C. insist that your supervisor give you his instructions in writing
   D. wait until your supervisor gives you more men before taking any action to carry out the assignment

45. Your crew consistently performs more work than the crew headed by another worker. The other worker tells you that the high performance of your crew makes his crew *look bad*.
Under these circumstances, it would be BEST for you to

   A. ignore the matter and have your crew continue working as before
   B. report the matter to your supervisor for disciplinary action
   C. slow your crew down somewhat to show the other man that you are willing to cooperate with him
   D. slow your crew down to the level of the other crew

46. Two of your men frequently argue with each other so that the work of your crew is disrupted.
You should FIRST

   A. attempt to find out why the men argue with each other
   B. speak to the two men privately regarding their possible transfer to another crew
   C. submit a report to your supervisor setting forth the facts
   D. tell both men that unless they stop arguing you will see that they are given below-standard service ratings

47. One of your men asks you to put him in for an above-standard service rating. His work has been good but it has not been above-standard.
You should tell the man that

   A. he has done good work but that in your judgment his work has not been above-standard
   B. if you recommend him for an above-standard service rating, you will have to do the same thing for most of the others in your crew
   C. you cannot discuss the matter with him but that you will discuss it with your supervisor
   D. you will speak to the other men in the crew and if no one objects you will recommend him for a higher service rating

48. You receive a memorandum from your supervisor in which he instructs you to make a large number of changes in the procedures for storing materials.
    The BEST way to bring these changes to the attention of your crew is to

    A. post the memorandum on the bulletin board where everyone can read it
    B. meet individually with each member of your staff to discuss the changes
    C. hold a meeting with your crew and explain the changes to them
    D. see to it that the memorandum is circulated to and initialled by each member of the crew

49. Although you have frequently spoken to one of your men regarding the proper way of lifting heavy objects, he persists in ignoring your instructions. He says that he knows the proper way of lifting, that you do not, and that he does not intend to hurt himself by following your instructions.
    Of the following, the BEST course of action for you to take is to

    A. assign the man to tasks which do not involve heavy lifting
    B. ignore the matter as long as the man does not hurt himself
    C. put your instructions on how to lift in writing and give a copy of your instructions to each man in the crew
    D. report the matter to your supervisor

50. You assign a man to take inventory of a certain item. The man gives you a figure which seems too high. Of the following, the BEST course of action for you to take is to

    A. accept the figure given to you by the man if he is willing to initial it
    B. accompany the man while he takes inventory again
    C. ask the man to take inventory again and tell him why
    D. take inventory yourself

KEY (CORRECT ANSWERS)

1. B	11. B	21. A	31. C	41. D
2. A	12. B	22. C	32. B	42. C
3. B	13. A	23. C	33. D	43. C
4. A	14. D	24. B	34. A	44. A
5. D	15. C	25. C	35. C	45. A
6. A	16. D	26. B	36. D	46. A
7. A	17. C	27. A	37. B	47. A
8. C	18. B	28. A	38. A	48. C
9. C	19. C	29. C	39. B	49. D
10. B	20. A	30. A	40. C	50. C

EXAMINATION SECTION
TEST 1

DIRECTIONS: Each question or incomplete statement is followed by several suggested answers or completions. Select the one that BEST answers the question or completes the statement. *PRINT THE LETTER OF THE CORRECT ANSWER IN THE SPACE AT THE RIGHT.*

1. The stock items on the purchase order should be the same as those on the shipment receipt at time of delivery.
   In general, it is BEST to check this at the time that the stock items are

   A. received in the storehouse
   B. ordered by the agency using the material
   C. issued by the storehouse personnel
   D. certified for payment

   1.____

2. Sawdust and shredded paper are materials that are generally used in which one of the following operations?

   A. Packing   B. Inventory
   C. Spraying   D. Transporting

   2.____

3. Storage areas with good air circulation and ventilation are generally considered

   A. *good,* only in hot and humid weather
   B. *good,* to retard mold growth
   C. *poor,* due to danger of fire
   D. *poor,* because of cleaning costs

   3.____

4. To get the best use from storage areas, it is usually BEST to use high ceilinged areas for storing

   A. heavy, bulky stock items
   B. lightweight stock items
   C. loose stock items in small bins
   D. extremely large-sized stock items

   4.____

5. The section of the storeroom that can carry the least weight should generally NOT be used for storing stock items that

   A. have a large size   B. have a small size
   C. are very heavy   D. are very light

   5.____

6. Where should you store unusually large and heavy stock items that are used very often?

   A. As close to the shipping and receiving areas as possible
   B. Away from work areas, such as shipping and receiving
   C. On hand trucks until the using agency asks for the item
   D. Only in storage areas which are outside the storehouse

   6.____

7. Which of the following would be MOST important in deciding how wide the space should be between cartons stacked in a storage area?

   7.____

A. Type of equipment that will be used to handle the stock
B. Size of the storage area
C. Number of employees in the storage area
D. How far the storage area is away from the receiving area

8. Stock items that might break, chip, or be crushed should be packed 8.____

   A. *tightly* with items touching each other
   B. *loosely* in a heavy wood container
   C. *tightly* with little movement allowed between items
   D. *tightly* with cushioning material between items

9. Suppose that some stock items delivered by truck are found to be damaged before they are unloaded. 9.____
   Which of the following actions would be BEST to take?

   A. Take the damaged stock and then give it out first to prevent further damage
   B. Refuse to take any damaged items
   C. Tell the driver of the truck to return the entire shipment
   D. Tell your supervisor about the damage so that he can take the necessary steps

10. It is dangerous to store gasoline because 10.____

    A. it can only be stored in specially constructed rooms in a storehouse
    B. it gives off vapors that can easily burn
    C. it can explode when moved around
    D. no one has found a safe way of storing gasoline

11. Gases are usually stored under pressure in steel cans. Which of the following is the LEAST dangerous practice? 11.____

    A. Allowing the cans to come in contact with electrical circuits
    B. Lifting the cans by their valves
    C. Allowing the cans to touch each other
    D. Keeping the valves on the cans open after the gas has been used up

12. Acids are a danger in storage because leakage may result in a sudden fire if contact is made with other chemicals. When storing acids, the one of the following practices which is INCORRECT is to 12.____

    A. keep them in heavy duty metal cans
    B. store them in isolated areas
    C. protect the containers against breakage
    D. keep flames or lit matches out of areas where acids are stored

13. Tape with a cellophane backing will become wrinkled and lumpy if stored in an area that is 13.____

    A. warm   B. cool   C. damp   D. very dry

14. To keep wooden furniture from warping and twisting, it should be stored in an area that is 14.____

    A. warm and dry   B. warm and damp
    C. cool and dry   D. cool and damp

15. Which one of the following items should NOT be stored in a very dry storage area? 15.____

    A. Soup cubes
    B. Baking soda
    C. Tea leaves
    D. Lettuce

16. Some food items can easily spoil. 16.____
    If they are packed in torn sacks or broken boxes, they should be stored

    A. in exactly the same way as other items
    B. just after fixing the sacks or boxes
    C. inside a bin in the storage area
    D. after spraying with DDT or another insect spray

17. Of the following items, which one is MOST likely to be damaged by insects? 17.____

    A. Iron pipes
    B. Rubber inner tubes
    C. Plastic tubing
    D. Grain products

18. Which one of the following items, when stored properly, has the SHORTEST storage life? 18.____

    A. Baked products
    B. Noodles
    C. Cornstarch
    D. Rolled oats

19. Which one of the following food items is LEAST likely to give off smells in a storehouse? 19.____

    A. Cheese
    B. Onions
    C. Fresh peaches
    D. Baking powder

20. The word *inventory* means the practice of counting all the stock items within each class of items. 20.____
    However, before an inventory can be done,

    A. the stock items must be thoroughly cleaned
    B. all stock items must be located and identified
    C. old stock items should be thrown away
    D. stock items that have been returned by the user should not be counted

---

KEY (CORRECT ANSWERS)

1.	A	11.	C
2.	A	12.	A
3.	B	13.	C
4.	B	14.	C
5.	C	15.	D
6.	A	16.	B
7.	A	17.	D
8.	D	18.	A
9.	D	19.	D
10.	B	20.	B

TEST 2

DIRECTIONS: Each question or incomplete statement is followed by several suggested answers or completions. Select the one that BEST answers the question or completes the statement. *PRINT THE LETTER OF THE CORRECT ANSWER IN THE SPACE AT THE RIGHT.*

1. *Pliers* may BEST be classified under

   A. food products
   B. tools
   C. office supplies
   D. machinery

   1.___

2. *White pine lumber* may BEST be classified under

   A. building materials
   B. laboratory materials
   C. safety materials
   D. seeds and plants

   2.___

3. *Linseed oil* may BEST be classified under

   A. drugs and chemicals
   B. painters' supplies
   C. building materials
   D. fuel and fuel oils

   3.___

4. *Ceiling tiles* may BEST be classified under

   A. office supplies
   B. hardware
   C. electrical supplies
   D. building materials

   4.___

5. *Floor finish remover* may BEST be classified under

   A. insecticides
   B. drugs
   C. machinery
   D. cleaning supplies

   5.___

6. *Arm slings* may BEST be classified under

   A. hospital supplies
   B. clothing
   C. school supplies
   D. office supplies

   6.___

7. *Staplers* may BEST be classified under

   A. office supplies
   B. laboratory supplies
   C. machinery and metals
   D. engineering supplies

   7.___

8. *Canvas stretcher* may BEST be classified under

   A. laboratory apparatus
   B. hospital supplies
   C. clothing
   D. tools

   8.___

9. *Switches* may BEST be classified under

   A. camera supplies
   B. vehicles
   C. electrical supplies
   D. pipes and pipe fittings

   9.___

10. *Bandages* may BEST be classified under

    A. laboratory equipment
    B. surgical instruments
    C. hospital supplies
    D. hose and belting

    10.___

Questions 11-15.

DIRECTIONS: Questions 11 through 15 are to be answered on the basis of the information given below.

LISTING OF PAPER
FOUND IN STOCKROOM A, ON APRIL 30

	Quantity Ordered by Stockroom A (in dozen reams)	Quantity in Stock Before Delivery (in dozen reams)	Cost Per Ream	Location of Stock in Stockroom
8 1/2"x11" Blue	17	5	$0.94	Bin A7
8 1/2"x11" Buff	8	3	$0.93	Bin A7
8 1/2"x11" Green	11	4	$0.95	Bin B4
8 1/2"x11" Pink	10	4	$0.93	Bin B4
8 1/2"x11" White	80	15	$0.86	Bin A8
8 1/2"x13" White	76	12	$1.02	Bin A8
8 1/2"x14" Blue	7	2	$1.19	Bin A7
8 1/2"x14" Buff	7	3	$1.18	Bin A7
8 1/2"x14" Green	5	2	$1.20	Bin B4
8 1/2"x14" Pink	8	4	$1.18	Bin B4
8 1/2"x14" White	110	28	$1.15	Bin A8
8 1/2"x14" Yellow	2	1	$1.23	Bin C6

11. How many reams of 8 1/2"x13" paper will there be in stock if only one-half of the amount ordered is delivered? _____ reams.

    A. 456 B. 600 C. 912 D. 1056

12. Suppose all ordered material is delivered.
    The bin that will have the MOST reams of paper is

    A. A7 B. A8 C. B4 D. C6

13. Suppose all ordered material has been delivered.
    What is the approximate value of all 8 1/2"x11" paper which is in Bin B4?

    A. $27 B. $171 C. $198 D. $327

14. How many reams of white paper of all sizes were ordered? _____ reams.

    A. 55 B. 266 C. 660 D. 3192

15. Before any of the orders were delivered, the following requests were filled and removed from the stockroom:
    2 dozen reams 8 1/2"x11" Blue; 2 dozen reams 8 1/2"x11" Green;
    7 dozen reams 8 1/2"x11" White; 5 dozen reams 8 1/2"x13" White;
    1 dozen reams 8 1/2"x14" Green; 13 dozen reams 8 1/2"x14" White.
    How many reams of paper were left in the stockroom after the above requests were filled?

    A. 30 B. 53 C. 636 D. 996

Questions 16-20.

DIRECTIONS: Questions 16 through 20 are to be answered SOLELY on the basis of the information given in the table below.

CONTROLLED DRUG A

Time Period	Purchase Order Number	Quantity Ordered	*Quantity Delivered by Vendor	Quantity Distributed during 2-week Period	Inventory Balance end of 2-Week Period
April 23-May 6	110,327	105 ounces	135 ounces	27 ounces	108 ounces
May 7-May 20	111,437	42 ounces	40 ounces	39 ounces	109 ounces
May 21-June 3	112,347	37 ounces	27 ounces	32 ounces	104 ounces
June 4-June 17	112,473	35 ounces	35 ounces	45 ounces	94 ounces
June 18-July 1	114,029	40 ounces	40 ounces	37 ounces	97 ounces

*Delivery is made on first day of time period.

16. The *difference* between Quantity Ordered and Quantity Delivered was greatest on Purchase Order Number

    A. 110,327   B. 111,437   C. 112,347   D. 112,473

17. The *difference* between the total number of ounces ordered and the total number of ounces delivered on April 23 through June 18 is _____ ounces.

    A. 17   B. 18   C. 19   D. 20

18. Suppose that average weekly usage was expected to be 26 ounces per week. Your supervisor has asked you to tell him whenever inventory balances get below a four-week level.
Under these conditions, you should have told your supervisor during the two-week period beginning

    A. April 23, May 21, June 4, June 18
    B. May 21, June 4, June 18
    C. May 21, June 18
    D. June 4, June 18

19. The GREATEST decreases in inventory balances happened between the two-week periods beginning

    A. April 23 and May 7   B. May 7 and May 21
    C. May 21 and June 4   D. June 4 and June 18

20. Suppose a new program has been started at your hospital and the weekly usage of Drug   20._____
A is expected to be 52 ounces per week.
If your supervisor must keep on hand a four-week supply, then the amount that should be delivered for the two-week period beginning on July 2 is _____ ounces.

    A. 52   B. 111   C. 208   D. 211

KEY (CORRECT ANSWERS)

1.	B	11.	B
2.	A	12.	B
3.	B	13.	D
4.	D	14.	D
5.	D	15.	C
6.	A	16.	A
7.	A	17.	B
8.	B	18.	D
9.	C	19.	C
10.	C	20.	B

TEST 3

DIRECTIONS: Each question or incomplete statement is followed by several suggested answers or completions. Select the one that BEST answers the question or completes the statement. *PRINT THE LETTER OF THE CORRECT ANSWER IN THE SPACE AT THE RIGHT.*

1. Suppose that 3-foot high boxes are to be stacked in one pile on a 4-inch platform. In addition, 4-inch thick separators are placed between each layer of boxes. Suppose that the ceiling is 22 feet high, and there must be at least 1 1/2 feet of space between the ceiling and the stacked boxes.
   What is the GREATEST number of boxes that can be stacked?

   A. 4 B. 5 C. 6 D. 7

   1.___

2. A part of a storeroom measures 14 1/2 feet by 6 1/4 feet.
   The number of square feet in this part is _____ square feet.

   A. 8 1/4 B. 20 3/4 C. 90 5/8 D. 94 3/4

   2.___

3. How many *cubic* feet of storage space would be taken up by 20 boxes, when each box measures 2 feet high, 2 feet wide, and 3 feet long? _____ cubic feet.

   A. 12 B. 27 C. 140 D. 240

   3.___

4. Suppose that a truckload of canned items has been unloaded. There are six rows of boxes with seven boxes in each row. Each box has two dozen cans in it.
   How many cans are there all together?

   A. 24 B. 144 C. 510 D. 1008

   4.___

5. Suppose that the average weekly use of tissue amounts to 180 rolls.
   At least how many boxes must be ordered for a 4-week period if there are 144 rolls in each box?

   A. 2 B. 3 C. 4 D. 5

   5.___

6. Suppose that a stockroom started the week with an initial supply of 3 gross of pencils and that one gross equals 144 pencils. After orders were filled, the stockroom had an inventory at the end of the week as follows: 2 gross of 4H pencils; 3 dozen 2B pencils; 1 1/2 dozen HB pencils; and 15H pencils.
   How many pencils were ordered?
   _____ pencils.

   A. 22 B. 45 C. 75 D. 97

   6.___

7. How many 18-inch pieces can be cut from 10 lengths of 8-foot glass tubing?
   _____ pieces.

   A. 47 B. 50 C. 53 D. 56

   7.___

8. Suppose a roll of wire is 27 feet 3 inches long. A piece of wire measuring 18 feet 9 inches in length is cut from the roll.
   What is the length of wire left on the roll? _____ feet _____ inches.

   A. 7; 3 B. 7; 6 C. 8; 3 D. 8; 6

   8.___

9. Suppose that 25% of a delivery of canned peaches was spoiled.
   If 36 cans were spoiled, then the delivery had a total of _____ cans.

   A. 9   B. 25   C. 144   D. 180

10. Suppose that a one-quart can of white flat ceiling paint weighs 5 pounds.
    What is the GREATEST number of quart cans that can be stored on a shelf that supports 167 pounds?
    _____ quart cans.

    A. 5   B. 33   C. 41   D. 67

11. Assume that the following orders were filled from a 55-gallon drum of oil: 9 pints, 7 pints, 2 quarts, 6 quarts, 3 gallons.
    How much oil is left in the drum?
    _____ gallons.

    A. 0   B. 8   C. 45   D. 48

12. Suppose a certain chemical can be given out only in one kilogram containers. 2.2 pounds equals 1 kilogram.
    The GREATEST number of kilograms that can be obtained from 100 pounds of this chemical is MOST NEARLY

    A. 41   B. 43   C. 45   D. 47

13. A truckload of supplies weighing 1 1/2 tons is unloaded by 5 workers in 2 hours. Suppose that the work is equally divided among the workers.
    How many pounds of supplies can be unloaded by each worker per hour?
    _____ pounds per hour.

    A. 150   B. 300   C. 450   D. 600

14. A room is 40 yards long and 15 yards wide. One square foot of floor can support 100 pounds.
    What is the GREATEST weight that can be supported by the floor in that room?

    A. 600   B. 5,400   C. 60,000   D. 540,000

15. Suppose that an empty storage area can be safely loaded with 324,000 lbs. of stock items.
    How many boxes can be stored in this area if each box has in it one dozen cans that weigh 3 pounds each?

    A. 8,500   B. 9,000   C. 9,500   D. 10,000

16. 18 boxes of oranges with 1000 oranges in each box are in a storehouse.
    How many orders of 1,440 oranges each can be filled completely?

    A. 10   B. 11   C. 12   D. 13

17. Suppose that the following 3 deliveries of dry cereal are made each day: 30 cartons with 60 boxes in each carton, 25 cartons with 60 boxes in each carton, and 20 cartons with 100 boxes in each carton.
    If daily orders total 400 boxes, how many more boxes must be delivered in order to have enough boxes for a 14-day supply?

A. 50   B. 100   C. 200   D. 300

18. Suppose that 11 pints of distilled water are used each day in the hospital laboratories and that a pint costs 7 cents.
    What would a 30-day supply of distilled water cost?
    About
    A. $23   B. $24   C. $25   D. $27

    18.____

19. If 2000 lbs. of salt costs $500, what does one pound cost?
    A. $.20   B. $.22   C. $.25   D. $.27

    19.____

20. The price of floor wax is 15 cents a quart. On orders of over 100 gallons, however, 2.5% is subtracted from the price of every quart in the order.
    What is the cost of 200 gallons of floor wax?
    A. $115   B. $117   C. $119   D. $121

    20.____

KEY (CORRECT ANSWERS)

1. C   11. D
2. C   12. C
3. D   13. B
4. D   14. D
5. D   15. B

6. C   16. C
7. B   17. D
8. D   18. A
9. C   19. C
10. B   20. B

TEST 4

DIRECTIONS: Each question or incomplete statement is followed by several suggested answers or completions. Select the one that BEST answers the question or completes the statement. *PRINT THE LETTER OF THE CORRECT ANSWER IN THE SPACE AT THE RIGHT.*

1. Employees who must lift and carry stock items should be careful to avoid injury. When an employee lifts or carries stock items, which of the following is the LEAST safe practice?

    A. Keep the legs straight and lift with the back muscles
    B. Keep the load as close to the body as possible
    C. Get a good grip on the object to be carried
    D. First determine if the item can be lifted and carried safely

    1.____

2. For warning and protection, the color red is usually used for

    A. indicating high temperature stockroom areas
    B. floor markings
    C. location of first aid supplies
    D. stop buttons, lights for barricades, and other dangerous locations

    2.____

3. Reporting rattles, squeaks, or other noises in equipment to your maintenance supervisor is

    A. *bad;* too much attention to squeaks like these keep important safety problems from being noticed
    B. *bad;* each person should oil and care for his own equipment
    C. *good;* these sounds may mean that the equipment should be fixed
    D. *good;* it shows the supervisor that you are a good worker

    3.____

4. If you often get cuts on your hands from handling different kinds of cartons and boxes, the BEST thing for you to do is

    A. keep from handling those kinds of cartons and boxes
    B. ask that better boxes and cartons be used
    C. toughen up your hands
    D. wear protective gloves

    4.____

5. A low, movable platform used for stacking material in a warehouse is called a *pallet*. When lifting and moving *pallets* with a forklift, how should a stockman place the forks?

    A. As wide apart as possible
    B. As close together as possible
    C. Close together and tilted forward
    D. Wide apart and tilted forward

    5.____

Questions 6-11.

DIRECTIONS: Questions 6 through 11 are to be answered ONLY on the information given in the following table.

RECORD OF INCOMING FREIGHT SHIPMENTS

Received	Purchase Order No.	Amount Prepaid	Amount To Be Collected	Shipper	No. of Items	Weight	Shippers' Catalog No.
1/7	9616	$15.10		Harding Grove Equip	14	170	28
1/12	3388		$ 2.00	People's Paper Inc.	10	50	091
1/12	8333		$106.19	Falls Office Supply	25	2500	701
2/2	7126		$ 9.00	Leigh Foods	175	4000	47
2/13	4964		$ 3.09	McBride Paper Co.	14	75	83
4/13	3380	$14.09		Central Hardware	14	1750	019
4/30	7261		$ 6.90	Northwestern Foods	121	2100	13
5/12	9166	$10.50		Harding Grove Equip.	15	50	36
5/17	6949		$ 4.19	Black's Paper Co.	40	65	743
5/31	6691		$ 20.00	Central Hardware	16	600	563
6/30	5388	$ 9.75		Harding Grove Equip.	15	15	420
6/30	8308		$ 22.50	Falls Office Supply	19	290	97
8/23	8553		$ 4.90	Tremont Paper Inc.	75	570	36
9/12	5338	$ 6.91		Northeast Hardware	51	901	071
10/15	6196	$12.00		Mobray Hardware	60	786	131

6. All items listed in the above table were delivered by   6.____

    A. U.S. mail   B. freight
    C. air express   D. ship

7. On what date was the LARGEST number of items received?   7.____

    A. 2/2   B. 2/13   C. 4/30   D. 5/17

8. If all items shipped by Falls Office Supply on 1/12 were of equal weight, how much did   8.____
each item weigh? _____ pounds.

    A. 10   B. 25   C. 100   D. 250

9. If the names of the shippers were put in alphabetical order, which of the following should be put after McBride Paper Company?   9.____

    A. Northeast Hardware   B. Leigh Foods
    C. Northwestern Foods   D. Mobray Hardware

10. What is the purchase order number for the Harding Grove Equipment shipment that was received on 5/12?   10.____

    A. 9166   B. 5388   C. 9616   D. 6691

11. All items that cost less than five dollars ($5.00) came from shippers of   11.____

    A. paper   B. foods
    C. hardware   D. office supplies

Questions 12-16.

DIRECTIONS: Questions 12 through 16 are to be answered SOLELY on the basis of the information contained in the following passage.

Floors in warehouses, storerooms, and shipping rooms must be strong enough to stay level under heavy loads. Unevenness of floors may cause boxes of materials to topple and fall. Safe floor load capacities and maximum heights to which boxes may be stacked should be posted conspicuously so all can notice it. Where material in boxes, containers, or cartons of the same weight is regularly stored, it is good practice to paint a horizontal line on the wall indicating the maximum height to which the material may be piled. A qualified expert should determine floor load capacity from the building plans, the age, and condition of the floor supports, the type of floor, and other related information.

Working aisles are those from which material is placed into and removed from storage. Working aisles are of two types: transportation aisles, running the length of the building, and cross aisles, running across the width of the building. Deciding on the number, width, and location of working aisles is important. While aisles are necessary and determine boundaries of storage areas, they reduce the space actually used for storage.

12. According to the passage above, how should safe floor load capacities be made known to employees?   12.____
    They should be

    A. given out to each employee
    B. given to supervisors only
    C. printed in large red letters
    D. posted so that they are easily seen

13. According to the passage above, floor load capacities should be determined by   13.____

    A. warehouse supervisors   B. the fire department
    C. qualified experts   D. machine operators

14. According to the above passage, transportation aisles   14.____

    A. run the length of the building
    B. run across the width of the building

C. are wider than cross aisles
D. are shorter than cross aisles

15. According to the passage above, working aisles tend to

    A. take away space that could be used for storage
    B. add to space that could be used for storage
    C. slow down incoming stock
    D. speed up outgoing stock

16. According to the passage above, unevenness of floors may cause

    A. overall warehouse deterioration
    B. piles of stock to fall
    C. materials to spoil
    D. many worker injuries

Questions 17-20.

DIRECTIONS: Questions 17 through 20 are to be answered SOLELY on the basis of the information contained in the following passage.

Planning for the unloading of incoming trucks is not easy since generally little or no advance notice of truck arrivals is received. The height of the floor of truck bodies and loading platforms sometimes are different; this makes necessary the use of special unloading methods. When available, hydraulic ramps compensate for the differences in platform and truck floor levels. When hydraulic ramps are not available, forklift equipment can sometimes be used, if the truck springs are strong enough to support such equipment. In a situation like this, the unloading operation does not differ much from unloading a railroad boxcar. In the cases where the forklift truck or a hydraulic pallet jack cannot be used inside the truck, a pallet dolly should be placed inside the truck, so that the empty pallet can be loaded close to the truck contents and rolled easily to the truck door and platform.

17. According to the passage above, unloading trucks is

    A. easy to plan since the time of arrival is usually known beforehand
    B. the same as loading a railroad boxcar
    C. hard to plan since trucks arrive without notice
    D. a very normal thing to do

18. According to the above passage, which materials handling equipment can make up for the difference in platform and truck floor levels?

    A. Hydraulic jacks   B. Hydraulic ramps
    C. Forklift trucks   D. Conveyors

19. According to the above passage, what materials handling equipment can be used when a truck cannot support the weight of forklift equipment?

    A. A pallet dolly   B. A hydraulic ramp
    C. Bridge plates   D. A warehouse tractor

20. Which is the BEST title for the above passage? 20.____
    A. Unloading Railroad Boxcars
    B. Unloading Motor Trucks
    C. Loading Rail Boxcars
    D. Loading Motor Trucks

KEY (CORRECT ANSWERS)

1.	B	11.	A
2.	D	12.	D
3.	C	13.	C
4.	D	14.	A
5.	A	15.	A
6.	B	16.	B
7.	A	17.	C
8.	C	18.	B
9.	D	19.	A
10.	A	20.	B

44

EXAMINATION SECTION
TEST 1

DIRECTIONS: Each question or incomplete statement is followed by several suggested answers or completions. Select the one that BEST answers the question or completes the statement. *PRINT THE LETTER OF THE CORRECT ANSWER IN THE SPACE AT THE RIGHT.*

Questions 1-10.

DIRECTIONS: Questions 1 through 10 are to be answered on the basis of Tables I and II below.

TABLE I
Building 5 Storeroom
Report of Dollar Cost of Stores Issued To
All Divisions in the Month of December

Divisions	11 Dept. Reports & Bulletins	12 Food Supplies	13 Motor Vehicle Supplies	14 Office Supplies	15 Printed Stationery & Forms	16 Printing & Reproducing Supplies	17 Small Tools & Implements
A	40		125	85	13	55	45
B	21		231	35	46	32	61
C	68	422		75	37	81	
D	81			83	98	77	91
E	32	168		69	51	43	

TABLE II
Building 5 Storeroom

Summary of Dollar Cost of Stores Issued
and Received and Balances, December

1 Supply Code	2 Balance Beginning of Month	3 Receipts From Vendors	4 Receipts From Storehouse A	5 Receipts From Storehouse B	6 Total Receipts	7 Total Issued	8 Balance
11	200	112	83	21	216	242	174
12	472	225	200	46	471	590	119
13	365	400			765	356	409
14	257	75	245	27	347	357	
15	245	89	152	36	277	255	277
16	281	104	190		294	288	287
17	197	32	110	40	182	197	182

1. The average value of small tools and implements received by Division C and E during the month of December

   A. is zero
   B. is approximately 78
   C. is 197
   D. cannot be determined from the information given

2. The division which received the GREATEST dollar value of stores in the month of December was

   A. A   B. B   C. C   D. D

3. The division which received the GREATEST number of items in all supply categories in December

   A. is A
   B. is B
   C. is D
   D. cannot be determined from the information given

4. In the column *Total Issued*, the entry which is INCORRECT is for

   A. Food Supplies
   B. Motor Vehicle Supplies
   C. Office Supplies
   D. Printed Stationery & Forms

5. In the column *Total Receipts*, the entry which is INCORRECT is for

   A. Department Reports & Bulletins
   B. Motor Vehicle Supplies
   C. Office Supplies
   D. Small Tools & Equipment

6. The Balance for Supply Code 14 has been omitted. This figure should be

   A. 10   B. 247   C. 367   D. 594

7. The Balance has been INCORRECTLY entered for

   A. Department Reports and Bulletins
   B. Food Supplies
   C. Printing and Reproducing Supplies
   D. Small Tools and Equipment

8. The dollar value of department reports and bulletins received from vendors in December exceeds that received from the storehouses by

   A. 8
   B. 12
   C. 29
   D. an indeterminate amount

9. For the classes of items received from Storehouse B during the month of December, the average dollar cost of these classes was MOST NEARLY

   A. 24   B. 34   C. 65   D. 170

10. One space is left blank in Column 4 of Table II. Judging only from the above tables, the MOST probable reason for this is that

   A. motor vehicle supplies were obtained from vendors only
   B. number 365 was inadvertently omitted from Column 4
   C. the figures for Columns 4 and 5 were included in Column 3
   D. the motor vehicle supply stock of Storehouse A is below the minimum stock level

11. If a physical inventory reveals a much smaller number of a particular item than is shown by the perpetual inventory record, it PROBABLY indicates

   A. a discontinuation of the stocking of the item
   B. a failure to record a withdrawal on the inventory record
   C. an unusual consumption of that particular item
   D. the non-delivery of an order for that item

12. The number of cartons measuring 3' x 3' x 2' which will be needed to pack 1,728 boxed items each measuring
    3" x 9" x 6" is

   A. 9   B. 18   C. 108   D. 192

13. Assume that a storehouse floor is 300 feet long, 200 feet wide, and 10 feet high. The total weight that the floor can hold is 3,000 tons.
    The safe floor load is _____ pounds per square foot.

   A. 100   B. 200   C. 300   D. 600

14. Seventy cartons, each 2 feet wide, 3 feet long, and 4 feet high, will require storage space measuring APPROXIMATELY _____ cubic yards.

   A. 24   B. 56   C. 63   D. 187

15. A certain item is stored in a crate measuring 3 feet in length, 4 feet in width, and 6 inches in height. It weighs 60 pounds.
    If the usable height of the storage area is twelve feet and if the safe floor load is 140 pounds per square foot, the number of crates which may be stacked right side up in a single column is

   A. 2   B. 5   C. 11   D. 24

16. You have to load 5,000 items on trucks each having a maximum load capacity of 2 1/2 tons. Each item weighs 20 pounds and takes up 2 cubic feet of storage space. Assume that the storage space in each truck has an area of 68 square feet and is 6 feet high. Without exceeding space or weight limitations, the SMALLEST number of trucks that could be used is

   A. 20   B. 25   C. 50   D. 63

17. Twenty pallet loads of a certain commodity have to be unloaded from a truck and moved to a certain location in the storehouse. It takes a forklift truck five minutes to unload two pallet loads at one time and place them on a trailer which can hold four pallet loads. It takes one tractor ten minutes to move five loaded trailers to the proper location in the storehouse.
Using one forklift truck, one tractor, and five trailers, and assuming no other time lost, the pallet loads can be unloaded and moved to the place where they will be stacked in

   A. 50 minutes
   B. 60 minutes
   C. 90 minutes
   D. 2 hours

17.____

18. A storeroom is 100 feet long and 26 feet wide. One aisle 8 feet wide runs the length of the storeroom. One aisle 4 feet wide runs the width of the storeroom.
If there were no other aisles, the number of square feet of usable storage space would be

   A. 1,696
   B. 1,728
   C. 2,280
   D. 2,568

18.____

19. A discount of 1% is given on all purchases of a certain item in quantities of 100 units or more. An additional discount of 1% is given on that portion of the purchase which exceeds 300.
If 450 units are purchased at a list price of $6.00, the total cost is

   A. $2,619
   B. $2,664
   C. $2,670
   D. $2,682

19.____

20. The amount of turpentine on hand is 27 1/2 gallons. One requisition is filled for 3 1/4 gallons, two additional requisitions are filled for 1 quart 8 ounces each, and five requisitions are filled for 2 pints 2 ounces each. The quantity of turpentine remaining after all these requisitions have been filled is

   A. 20 gal. 3 qts. 1 pt.
   B. 21 gal. 3 qts. 1 pt.
   C. 22 gal. 1 qt. 6 oz.
   D. 22 gal. 1 1/2 qts. 10 oz.

20.____

21. If the average height of the stacks in your section of the storehouse is 9 1/2 feet, the area which will be occupied by 11,400 cubic feet of supplies is APPROXIMATELY _____ square feet.

   A. 100
   B. 120
   C. 1,000
   D. 1,200

21.____

22. Letting oily rags or dust cloths accumulate in a closet is a fire hazard PRINCIPALLY because of the possibility of

   A. a match or cigarette being dropped
   B. fire spreading from other areas
   C. spontaneous combustion
   D. their use in inflammable areas

22.____

23. Assume that you have depleted your entire stock of 1,692 units of a certain item by sending 524 units to one location and dividing the remainder of the stock equally among 16 other locations.
The number of units that was sent to each of these 16 locations was

   A. 48
   B. 73
   C. 116
   D. 168

23.____

24. Of the following, the MOST advisable way to increase storage space is to

    A. decrease stock supplies below minimum
    B. eliminate items that are infrequently used
    C. stack to maximum height
    D. utilize aisle space

25. In a large storehouse, an area with a high ceiling is ordinarily BEST for storing items which are

    A. irregular in shape, heavy, and on skids
    B. irregular in shape, light, and on pallets
    C. rectangular in shape and on pallets
    D. rectangular in shape and on skids

26. The term *legal-size* refers to paper which is generally _____ than letter-size paper.

    A. longer
    B. longer and narrower
    C. longer and wider
    D. wider

27. A *trier* is a device used for

    A. sampling   B. sealing   C. stamping   D. weighing

28. Of the following items, the one for which the MOST care should be taken to prevent moth damage is

    A. nylon brushes
    B. orlon fabrics
    C. pianos
    D. shoes

29. Circulation of air is LEAST desirable for

    A. batteries   B. cement   C. linoleum   D. paint

30. There are five units of a circular piece of equipment which weighs 9,000 pounds and has a solid circular base and a solid circular top each 4 feet in diameter.
    In MOST cases, the BEST way to store these five units would be to

    A. crate them and place one next to the other
    B. crate them and stack them two high
    C. place one next to the other without crating
    D. stack them two high without crating

31. You have just received a shipment of 500 packages, each 2" long, 1' wide, and 1/2' high, and each weighing 25 pounds. You are going to store them in an area 10' by 10' by 10' where the safe floor load is 100 pounds per square foot. The number of these packages which may be safely stored right side up is

    A. 100   B. 200   C. 400   D. 500

32. Assume that you have several men and the following equipment available: two forklift trucks, one tractor, five trailers, and two handtrucks.
    In order to move twenty pallet loads 200 yards in a storehouse, it would be MOST advisable for you to use the

A. forklift trucks
B. tractor and the trailers
C. tractor, the trailers, and the forklift trucks
D. tractor, the trailers, the handtrucks, and one fork-lift truck

33. Of the following, the MOST suitable temperature for the storage of fresh milk is   33.____

    A. 0° F   B. 16° F   C. 32° F   D. 48° F

34. Of the following, the MOST suitable temperature for the storage of frozen meats is   34.____

    A. 0° F   B. 16° F   C. 32° F   D. 48° F

35. An isolated section of the storehouse has just been made available for your use. It has all the facilities available in other sections of the storehouse, except that it is distant from shipping and receiving areas and all centers of activity.   35.____
    Of the following items in the storehouse, the one which should ordinarily receive priority consideration for storage in such a section is

    A. codeine   B. flour   C. gasoline   D. machinery

36. Assume that you have to move 100 pallets from one location in the warehouse to another about 20 feet away. Which of the following would you need to do the job MOST efficiently?   36.____

    A. Conveyor
    B. Forklift truck
    C. Forklift truck, tractor, trailers
    D. Four-wheel handtruck, portable elevator

37. Of the following, the QUICKEST and EASIEST way to move thirty pallet loads of material 800 feet and then stack then is to use a   37.____

    A. forklift truck and a tractor-trailer train
    B. forklift truck and a crane
    C. portable elevator
    D. portable elevator and 6 handtrucks

38. The BEST measure of the effectiveness of a tractor-trailer combination is the   38.____

    A. amount of power used per day
    B. amount of stock that can be moved in a day
    C. amount of stock that can be moved in each trip
    D. number of miles which can be covered in a day

39. As compared to a conventional counterbalance design fork-lift truck, a straddle arm fork-lift truck with the same lifting capacity will USUALLY weigh   39.____

    A. approximately the same   B. less
    C. much more   D. slightly more

40. The one of the following which is NOT of major importance in determining the location of an item in a storehouse is   40.____

    A. difficulty of handling   B. fire hazard
    C. floor strength   D. purpose for which used

41. A usually competent stockman under your supervision has complained to you that a newly employed assistant stockman knows nothing about handling or storing stock.
Of the following, the MOST advisable course of action for you to take is to

   A. advise the stockman not to interfere
   B. arrange for a transfer of the new worker
   C. ask the stockman whether he is willing to assist in on-the-job training
   D. tell the new worker that he will have to do better

42. Assume that an employee tells you that you have made an error in issuing certain instructions. You do not believe this to be true.
The MOST appropriate action for you to take in MOST cases is to

   A. ask him to follow the instructions as they were given
   B. get some of the other employees together to discuss the matter
   C. have him explain why he believes it to be an error
   D. tell him to do it any way he wants to, as long as the job gets done

43. In planning a large operation involving the movement and handling of stock, it would be MOST desirable for a storekeeper to

   A. confer only with his supervisor and other storekeepers
   B. discuss the matter only with his more capable subordinates
   C. have his subordinates participate in the planning
   D. rely solely upon his own judgment and knowledge

44. As a storekeeper, you find that routine and clerical duties greatly decrease the time you can spend in supervising your subordinates.
Of the following, you should FIRST attempt to

   A. delegate some of your supervisory duties to the most qualified subordinates
   B. have an assistant assigned to take over some of your duties
   C. reduce the number of persons under your supervision
   D. turn over some of the routine and clerical work to your subordinates

45. As a storekeeper in charge of a storehouse, you find that there is a considerable backlog in the filling of requisitions, and you have received complaints from using agencies Of the following, the MOST advisable course of action for you to take FIRST is to

   A. advise the using agencies that they must wait their turn
   B. determine the factors causing the backlog
   C. take appropriate disciplinary action where indicated
   D. work out plans for removing the backlog

46. It is necessary for you to assign one of the men in the storehouse to the main office for two weeks to work on records.
Which of the following men should be chosen?

   A. Al is the best at records work, but he is very reluctant to go.
   B. Ben is next to Al in ability of records work and is interested in going, but he is so likeable that you are afraid the main office will want to keep him permanently.

C. Carl is next to Ben in ability at records work, but it would be a great hardship for him to go because of his time schedule and the traveling.
D. Dan has little ability at records work, but he has not done well in your division and he is anxious to try working in the main office.

47. An employee under your supervision comes to you to complain about an assignment you have made. You consider the matter to be unimportant, but it seems to be very important to him. He is excited and very angry.
Of the following, the MOST advisable action to take FIRST is to

   A. let him talk until he *gets it off his chest*
   B. refuse to talk to him until he has *cooled down*
   C. show him at once how unimportant the matter is
   D. tell him to talk it over with the other employees

48. Of the following, the BEST reason why accuracy in keeping records should be considered more important than speed is that

   A. most employees cannot work rapidly and also be accurate
   B. most supervisors insist upon accurate work, while very few pay attention to speed
   C. much time may be lost correcting or redoing work that is done too hastily
   D. speedy workers are usually inaccurate

49. A fistfight develops between two stockmen under your supervision.
The MOST advisable course of action for you to take FIRST is to

   A. call the police
   B. have the other workers pull them apart
   C. order them to stop
   D. step between the two men

50. You have assigned some difficult and unusual work to one of your most experienced and competent subordinates.
If you notice that he is doing the work incorrectly, you should

   A. assign the work to another employee
   B. reprimand him in private
   C. show him immediately how the work should be done
   D. wait until the job is completed and then correct his errors

KEY (CORRECT ANSWERS)

1. A	11. B	21. D	31. D	41. C
2. C	12. A	22. C	32. A	42. C
3. D	13. A	23. B	33. C	43. C
4. D	14. C	24. C	34. A	44. D
5. B	15. D	25. C	35. C	45. B
6. B	16. B	26. A	36. B	46. B
7. B	17. B	27. A	37. A	47. A
8. A	18. B	28. C	38. B	48. C
9. B	19. B	29. B	39. B	49. C
10. A	20. C	30. C	40. D	50. C

EXAMINATION SECTION
TEST 1

DIRECTIONS: Each question or incomplete statement is followed by several suggested answers or completions. Select the one that BEST answers the question or completes the statement. *PRINT THE LETTER OF THE CORRECT ANSWER IN THE SPACE AT THE RIGHT.*

1. Assume that your warehouse received a shipment of 600 articles. A sample of 60 articles was inspected. Of this sample, one article was wholly defective, and four articles were partly defective. On the basis of this sampling, you would expect the total number of defective articles in this shipment to be

    A. 5   B. 10   C. 40   D. 50

2. The stock inventory card for paint, white, flat, one gallon, has the following entries:

Date	Received	Shipped	Balance
April 12	-	25	75
April 13	50	75	
April 14	-	10	
April 15	25	-	
April 16	-	10	

    The balance on hand at the close of business on April 15 should be

    A. 40   B. 45   C. 55   D. 65

Questions 3-8.

DIRECTIONS: For each Question 3 through 8, select the choice whose meaning is MOST NEARLY the same as that of the numbered item.

3. ADJACENT

    A. near   B. critical   C. sensitive   D. sharp

4. CONSOLIDATE

    A. divide in half   B. direct
    C. agree   D. unite

5. DETERIORATE

    A. decorate   B. prevent   C. regulate   D. worsen

6. EXPEDITE

    A. label carefully   B. process promptly
    C. represent   D. terminate

7. NEGLIGENT

    A. careless   B. painful   C. pleasant   D. positive

8. VENDOR

    A. customer   B. inspector   C. manager   D. seller

2 (#1)

Questions 9-12.

DIRECTIONS: Questions 9 through 12 are to be answered SOLELY on the basis of the following passage.

Several special factors must be taken into account in selecting trucks to be used in a warehouse that stores food in freezer and cold storage rooms. Since gasoline fumes may contaminate the food, the trucks should be powered by electricity, not by gasoline. The trucks must be specially equipped to operate in the extreme cold of freezer rooms. The equipment must be dependable, for if a truck breaks down while transporting frozen food from a railroad car to the freezer of a warehouse, this expensive merchandise will quickly spoil. Finally, since cold storage and freezer rooms are expensive to operate, commodities must be stored close together, and the aisles between the rows of commodities must be as narrow as possible. Therefore, the trucks must be designed to work even in narrow aisles.

9. Of the following, the BEST title for the above passage is:

    A. Expenses Involved in Operating a Freezer or Cold Storage Room
    B. How to Prevent Food Spoilage in Freezer and Cold Storage Rooms
    C. Selecting the Best Trucks to Use in a Food Storage Warehouse
    D. The Problem of Contamination of Food by Gasoline Fumes

10. According to the above passage, electrically powered trucks should be used for moving food in freezer and cold storage rooms chiefly because they

    A. are cheaper to operate than gasoline powered trucks
    B. are dependable
    C. can operate in extremes of heat and cold
    D. do not produce fumes which may contaminate food

11. Trucks designed for use in narrow aisles should be used in freezer and cold storage rooms because

    A. commodities are placed close together in freezer rooms to save space
    B. commodities spoil quickly if the space between aisles in the freezer is too wide
    C. narrow aisle trucks are more dependable
    D. narrow aisle trucks are run by electricity

12. According to the above passage, all of the following factors should be taken into account in selecting a truck for use to transport frozen food into and within a cold storage room EXCEPT

    A. ability to operate in extreme cold
    B. dependability
    C. the weight of the truck
    D. whether or not the truck emits exhaust fumes

Questions 13-22.

DIRECTIONS: For Questions 13 through 22, choose from the given classifications the one under which the item is MOST likely to be found in general stock catalogs.

13. *Columnar pads* may BEST be classified under 13.____

    A. dry goods, textiles, and floor covering
    B. hospital and surgical supplies
    C. recreational supplies and equipment
    D. stationery and office supplies

14. *Trowels* may BEST be classified under 14.____

    A. dry goods and textiles
    B. hand tools and agricultural implements
    C. household supplies
    D. surgical supplies

15. *Collanders* may BEST be classified under 15.____

    A. building materials   B. kitchen utensils
    C. motor vehicle parts   D. plumbing supplies

16. *Litmus paper* may BEST be classified under 16.____

    A. laboratory supplies   B. sewing supplies
    C. stationery and supplies   D. textiles

17. *Pipettes* may BEST be classified under 17.____

    A. hardware
    B. hospital and laboratory supplies
    C. kitchen utensils and tableware
    D. plumbing fixtures and parts

18. *Carbon tetrachloride* may BEST be classified under 18.____

    A. brushes
    B. clothing and textiles
    C. drugs and chemicals
    D. toilet articles and accessories

19. *Curry powder* may BEST be classified under 19.____

    A. drugs and chemicals
    B. food and condiments
    C. paints and supplies
    D. surgical and dental supplies

20. *Wing nuts* may BEST be classified under 20.____

    A. food and condiments   B. hardware supplies
    C. household utensils   D. sewing supplies

21. *Shears* may BEST be classified under 21.____

    A. agricultural implements   B. clothing and textiles
    C. electrical parts   D. furniture

22. *Chambray* may BEST be classified under

   A. canned goods, food, and miscellaneous groceries
   B. brooms and brushes
   C. drugs and chemicals
   D. dry goods and textiles

23. Four city-owned trucks, all the same make, model, and capacity, were dispatched on round trips each with a 120 gallon tank full of gas. After Truck A had traveled 225 miles, his tank was 1/4 full. After Truck B had traveled 120 miles, his tank was 1/2 full. After Truck C had traveled 75 miles, his tank was 3/4 full. After Truck D had traveled 300 miles, his tank was empty. Which truck had the POOREST average mileage per gallon of gas?
   Truck

   A. A   B. B   C. C   D. D

24. Assume that you receive a shipment of 9 boxes of paper towels. Each box contains 6 dozen packages. Each package contains 200 paper towels. The total cost of the shipment of boxes is $64.80. The unit of issue for paper towels is the package.
   The unit cost of the paper towels is

   A. $0.10   B. $0.90   C. $1.20   D. $7.20

25. One shipment of 70 shovels costs $140. A second shipment of 130 shovels costs $208. The average cost per shovel for both shipments is MOST NEARLY

   A. $1.60   B. $1.75   C. $2.00   D. $2.50

KEY (CORRECT ANSWERS)

1. D		11. A	
2. D		12. C	
3. A		13. D	
4. D		14. B	
5. D		15. B	
6. B		16. A	
7. A		17. B	
8. D		18. C	
9. C		19. B	
10. D		20. B	

21. A
22. D
23. B
24. A
25. B

TEST 2

DIRECTIONS: Each question or incomplete statement is followed by several suggested answers or completions. Select the one that BEST answers the question or completes the statement. *PRINT THE LETTER OF THE CORRECT ANSWER IN THE SPACE AT THE RIGHT.*

Questions 1-5.

DIRECTIONS: Questions 1 through 5 show items that have been requisitioned by city agencies. In each group of four items, there is one item which has NOT been described in sufficient detail to enable the storekeeper or his subordinates to fill the order promptly from the variety of stock on hand. For each question, select the item that has pertinent, important information missing.

1. A. Fuses, auto, glass, 25 volts
   B. Ladders, extension, 2 sections, 30', metal
   C. Paint, interior, white, 1 gallon can, flat
   D. Stoppers, rubber, solid, white, nickel plated, brass ring, 1"

2. A. Aspirin, U.S.P., 1 grain - 1,000 in bottle
   B. Blotters, desk, 120 lb. stock, 24" x 38", green
   C. Folders, file, manila, 1/3 cut
   D. Nutmeg, ground, 1 lb. container

3. A. Safety pins, brass, nickel plated, size 2
   B. Sheets, bed, cotton, white
   C. Thermometer, oven, 100/600 degree F, enamel
   D. Toothbrush, adult size, nylon bristle

4. A. Pencil, black lead, #2, general office use, with eraser
   B. Stencil, dry-process, blue, legal size #2960
   C. Tape, cellulose, 1/2 in. x 1296 in., core diameter 1 in.
   D. Typewriter ribbon, standard, black record

5. A. Fruits, canned, peaches
   B. Milk, processed, dry powdered, whole, bulk
   C. Olives, stuffed, 16 oz. bottle, 12 bottles to case
   D. Sugar, granulated, 100 lb. bag

6. The deterioration of some items is accelerated when temperature exceeds 70° F and humidity is greater than 40 percent.
   Of the following, the item that would be LEAST affected by increases of temperature and humidity above these amounts is

   A. bristle brushes   B. cellophane tape
   C. rice   D. typewriter ribbons

7. The storage life of many items varies according to temperature and humidity. To gain maximum storage life, the one of the following items which should be stored in an area having a temperature of 55° F with 50 percent relative humidity is

A. clothing B. steel parts
C. tires D. x-ray film

8. A shipment of 200 creosote logs 12" in diameter with lengths varying from 20' to 30' each will arrive on flatbed trucks and are to be stored. The mode of power to be employed to move the logs from the flatbeds to an outdoor storage area is a warehouse crane.
To avoid slippage, the pulley ropes or chains should be attached to the logs with a

   A. double basket sling
   B. double choker sling with hooks attached
   C. four leg bridle sling with spliced eyes
   D. hammock sling

Questions 9-12.

DIRECTIONS: Questions 9 through 12 represent items appearing on requisitions received in a storehouse. Assume that you have a wide variety of each item named. Some important information is missing from each description. Without this missing information (NOT code number or account number), it would be difficult to select the appropriate item from the variety in stock. From the choices given, select the one that represents the missing additional information that would be MOST important and helpful in filling each requisition.

9. PAPER, mimeograph, 100% sulphite sub 20, white

   A. bond or onionskin B. ruled or unruled
   C. size of paper D. two or three holes

10. NEEDLES, hand sewing, 20 to package

    A. cost B. metallic composition
    C. purpose D. size

11. SCREWS, wood, gross in box, brass, 1/2", No. 2

    A. round or flat head
    B. size of bolt
    C. type of lumber for which used
    D. type of metal of which made

12. THREAD, SPOOL COTTON, hand sewing, 6 cord, 500 yd., one dozen in box, #60

    A. color of thread
    B. size of needle's eye
    C. type of fabric to be sewn
    D. diameter of spool

13. Of the following, the LEAST appropriate preservative to apply to a wooden ladder is

    A. clear varnish B. lacquer
    C. linseed oil D. paint

14. Of the following, the type of lighting that is MOST efficient for maximum illumination in an equipment maintenance area is

    A. *incandescent* (direct)
    B. *incandescent* (general diffusing)
    C. *fluorescent* (direct)
    D. *fluorescent* (semi-direct)

15. Of the following chemicals, the one which is MOST hazardous and requires extra precautionary storage and handling methods is

    A. citric acid
    B. hydrogen peroxide
    C. nitric acid
    D. oxalic acid

16. You are informed that several cases of canned condensed milk have spoiled and you are assigned to seek the cause and find a remedy.
    In the absence of any specific information, which of the following is MOST likely to have been the cause of this spoilage?

    A. Improper rotation of stock
    B. Adequate ventilation
    C. Insect infestation
    D. Insufficient heat

17. Inventory records are essential to efficient warehouse operations.
    Of the following purposes served by inventory records, the one which is of LEAST importance to warehouse operating personnel is the

    A. establishment of quantity controls
    B. estimation of present values of items
    C. identification of stock items
    D. location of stock items

18. When in storage, the one of the following which it is MOST important to sprinkle periodically with naphthalene flakes is

    A. canvas cots
    B. cotton towels
    C. manila rope
    D. wool blankets

19. Generally, the time required to fill a requisition will be LEAST affected by the _____ of the item requisitioned.

    A. amount
    B. dimensions
    C. length of the description
    D. location

20. Of the following, the BEST procedure to follow in order to insure that a laborer has understood instructions that you have just given to him is to

    A. ask the laborer if he has any questions about the instructions
    B. have the laborer explain the instructions to you
    C. repeat the key points of the instructions to the laborer
    D. write out the instructions and give them to the laborer

21. You have been assigned several newly-appointed inexperienced stockmen and laborers whose performance in inadequate.
Of the following, the BEST course of action is to

    A. commence a training program for all employees under your supervision
    B. provide special guidance to those employees whose performance is inadequate
    C. do a work simplification study
    D. take steps to improve morale through incentive awards

21.____

22. Assume that one of your subordinates knows more about a certain aspect of the work than you do. You notice that many of the workers go to him rather than to you for advice on this aspect of the work.
You should

    A. delegate your authority and responsibility in this aspect of the work to this subordinate
    B. direct the workers to bring all questions about the work to you
    C. permit this to continue as long as it does not interfere with the work of this subordinate
    D. tell this subordinate that he is to refer any requests for information to you

22.____

23. Assume that about 11 A.M. one of your stockmen reports to you that one of the assistant stockmen appears to be drunk and is creating a disturbance in the warehouse. The MOST appropriate action for you to take FIRST in this situation is to

    A. ask the stockman to bring the assistant stockman who appears to be drunk to your office
    B. call the police department for assistance
    C. go with the stockman to investigate the matter
    D. report the matter to your supervisor

23.____

24. Assume that you have received an anonymous letter alleging that the crew of one of your delivery trucks has been observed parked at a certain location for periods of one hour or more on several occasions. This location is not in the vicinity of any agency where your crew would be required to make deliveries.
In this situation, the MOST appropriate action for you to take is to

    A. break up the crew by reassigning each member to other duties
    B. follow the crew for several days as they are making deliveries
    C. ignore the letter since it is anonymous
    D. interview each member of the crew privately to find out what he has to say about the allegation

24.____

25. Assume that one of your subordinates has gotten into the habit of regularly and routinely referring every small problem which arises in his work to you.
In order to help him overcome this habit, it is generally MOST advisable for you to

   A. advise him that you do not have time to discuss each problem with him and that he should do whatever he wants
   B. ask your subordinate for his solution and approve any satisfactory approach that he suggests
   C. refuse to discuss such routine problems with him
   D. tell him that he should consider looking for another position if he does not feel competent to solve such routine problems

25.____

KEY (CORRECT ANSWERS)

1.	A	11.	A
2.	C	12.	A
3.	B	13.	D
4.	D	14.	C
5.	A	15.	C
6.	A	16.	A
7.	D	17.	B
8.	B	18.	D
9.	C	19.	C
10.	D	20.	B

21.	B
22.	C
23.	C
24.	D
25.	B

READING COMPREHENSION
UNDERSTANDING AND INTERPRETING WRITTEN MATERIAL
EXAMINATION SECTION
TEST 1

DIRECTIONS: Each question or incomplete statement is followed by several suggested answers or completions. Select the one that BEST answers the question or completes the statement. *PRINT THE LETTER OF THE CORRECT ANSWER IN THE SPACE AT THE RIGHT.*

Questions 1-6.

DIRECTIONS: Questions 1 through 6 are to be answered SOLELY on the basis of the information contained in the following passage.

Duplicating is the process of making a number of identical copies of letters, documents, etc. from an original. Some duplicating processes make copies directly from the original document. Other duplicating processes require the preparation of a special master, and copies are then made from the master. Four of the most common duplicating processes are stencil, fluid, offset, and xerox.

In the stencil process, the typewriter is used to cut the words into a master called a stencil. Drawings, charts, or graphs can be cut into the stencil using a stylus. As many as 3,500 good-quality copies can be reproduced from one stencil. Various grades of finished paper from inexpensive mimeograph to expensive bond can be used.

The fluid process is a good method of copying from 50 to 125 good-quality copies from a master, which is prepared with a special dye. The master is placed on the duplicator, and special paper with a hard finish is moistened and then passed through the duplicator. Some of the dye on the master is dissolved, creating an impression on the paper. The impression becomes lighter as more copies are made; and once the dye on the master is used up, a new master must be made.

The offset process is the most adaptable office duplicating process because this process can be used for making a few copies or many copies. Masters can be made on paper or plastic for a few hundred copies, or on metal plates for as many as 75,000 copies. By using a special technique called photo-offset, charts, photographs, illustrations, or graphs can be reproduced on the master plate. The offset process is capable of producing large quantities of fine, top-quality copies on all types of finished paper.

The xerox process reproduces an exact duplicate from an original. It is the fastest duplicating method because the original material is placed directly on the duplicator, eliminating the need to make a special master. Any kind of paper can be used. The xerox process is the most expensive duplicating process; however, it is the best method of reproducing small quantities of good-quality copies of reports, letters, official documents, memos, or contracts.

1. Of the following, the MOST efficient method of reproducing 5,000 copies of a graph is
   A. stencil   B. fluid   C. offset   D. Xerox

2. The offset process is the MOST adaptable office duplicating process because
   A. it is the quickest duplicating method
   B. it is the least expensive duplicating method
   C. it can produce a small number or large number of copies
   D. a softer master can be used over and over again

3. Which one of the following duplicating processes uses moistened paper?
   A. Stencil   B. Fluid   C. Offset   D. Xerox

4. The fluid process would be the BEST process to use for reproducing
   A. five copies of a school transcript
   B. fifty copies of a memo
   C. five hundred copies of a form letter
   D. five thousand copies of a chart

5. Which one of the following duplicating processes does NOT require a special master?
   A. Fluid   B. Xerox   C. Offset   D. Stencil

6. Xerox is NOT used for all duplicating jobs because
   A. it produces poor-quality copies
   B. the process is too expensive
   C. preparing the master is too time-consuming

Questions 7-10.

DIRECTIONS: Questions 7 through 10 are to be answered SOLELY on the basis of the information contained in the following passage.

City government is committed to providing a safe and healthy work environment for all city employees. An effective agency safety program reduces accidents by educating employees about the types of careless acts which can cause accidents. Even in an office, accidents can happen. If each employee is aware of possible safety hazards, the number of accidents on the job can be reduced.

Careless use of office equipment can cause accidents and injuries. For example, file cabinet drawers which are filled with papers can be so heavy that the entire cabinet could tip over from the weight of one open drawer.

The bottom drawers of desks and file cabinets should never be left open since employees could easily trip over open drawers and injure themselves.

When reaching for objects on a high shelf, an employee should use a strong, sturdy object such as a step stool to stand on. Makeshift platforms made out of books, papers, or boxes can easily collapse. Even chairs can slide out from under foot, causing serious injury.

Even at an employee's desk, safety hazards can occur. Frayed or cut wires should be repaired or replaced immediately. Typewriters which are not firmly anchored to the desk or table could fall, causing injury.

Smoking is one of the major causes of fires in the office. A lighted match or improperly extinguished cigarette thrown into a wastebasket filled with paper could cause a major fire with possible loss of life. Where smoking is permitted, ashtrays should be used. Smoking is particularly dangerous in offices where flammable chemicals are used.

7. The goal of an effective safety program is to 7.____
   A. reduce office accidents
   B. stop employees from smoking on the job
   C. encourage employees to continue their education
   D. eliminate high shelves in offices

8. Desks and file cabinets can become safety hazards when 8.____
   A. their drawers are left open
   B. they are used as wastebaskets
   C. they are makeshift
   D. they are not anchored securely to the floor

9. Smoking is especially hazardous when it occurs 9.____
   A. near exposed wires
   B. in a crowded office
   C. in an area where flammable chemicals are used
   D. where books and papers are stored

10. Accidents are likely to occur when 10.____
    A. employees' desks are cluttered with books and papers
    B. employees are not aware of safety hazards
    C. employees close desk drawers
    D. step stools are used to reach high objects

Questions 11-18.

DIRECTIONS: Questions 11 through 18 are to be answered SOLELY on the basis of the information contained in the following passage.

The telephone directory is made up of two books. The first book consists of the introductory section and the alphabetical listing of names section. The second book is the classified directly (also known as the yellow pages). Many people who are familiar with one book do not realize how useful the other can be. The efficient office worker should become familiar with both books in order to make the best use of this important source of information.

The introductory section gives general instructions for finding numbers in the alphabetical listing and classified directory. This section also explains how to use the telephone company's many services, including the operator and information services, gives examples of charges for local and long distance calls, and lists area codes for the entire country. In addition, this section provides a useful postal zip code map.

The alphabetical listing of names section lists the names, addresses, and telephone numbers of subscribers in an area. Guide names, or *telltales*, are on the top corner of each page. These guide names indicate the first and last name to be found on that page. *Telltales* help locate any particular name quickly. A cross-reference spelling is also given to help locate names which are spelled several different ways. City, state, and federal government agencies are listed under the major government heading. For example, an agency of the federal government would be listed under *United States Government*.

The classified directory, or yellow pages, is a separate book. In this section are advertising services, public transportation line maps, shopping guides, and listing of businesses arranged by the type of product or services they offer. This book is most useful when looking for the name or phone number of a business when all that is known is the type of product offered and the address, or when trying to locate a particular type of business in an area. Businesses listed in the classified directory can usually be found in the alphabetical listing of names section. When the name of the business is known, you will find the address or phone number more quickly in the alphabetical listing of names section.

11. The introductory section provides
    A. shopping guides
    B. government listings
    C. business listings
    D. information services

12. Advertising services would be found in the
    A. introductory section
    B. alphabetical listing of names section
    C. classified directory
    D. information services

13. According to the information in the above passage for locating government agencies, the Information Office of the Department of Consumer Affairs of New York city government would be alphabetically listed FIRST under
    A. *I* for Information Offices
    B. *D* for Department of Consumer Affairs
    C. *N* for New York City
    D. *G* for government

14. When the name of a business is known, the QUICKEST way to find the phone number is to look in the
    A. classified directory
    B. introductory section
    C. alphabetical listing of names section
    D. advertising service section

15. The QUICKEST way to find the phone number of a business when the type of service a business offers and its address is known is to look in the
    A. classified directory
    B. alphabetical listing of names section
    C. introductory section
    D. information service

16. What is a *telltale*?
    A(n)
    A. alphabetical listing
    B. guide name
    C. map
    D. cross-reference listing

17. The BEST way to find a postal zip code is to look in the
    A. classified directory
    B. introductory section
    C. alphabetical listing of names section
    D. government heading

18. To help find names which have several different spellings, the telephone directory provides
    A. cross-reference spelling
    B. *telltales*
    C. spelling guides
    D. advertising services

Questions 19-24.

DIRECTIONS: Questions 19 through 24 are to be answered SOLELY on the basis of the information contained in the following instructions on sweeping.

SWEEPING

All sweeping must be done with damp sawdust, which is used to prevent the raising of dust when sweeping platforms and mezzanines. Soak sawdust thoroughly in a bucket of water for two to three hours before use. Drain before use so that no stains are left on concrete from excess water. In order to keep sawdust moist while being used, spread for an area of 120 feet in advance of actual sweeping. Never sweep sawdust over drains. To assure good footing, do not spread it on stairways or on damp or wet floor areas.

19. Dampened sawdust should be used when
    A. scrapping   B. dusting   C. sweeping   D. mopping

20. Of the following procedures, which is the CORRECT order to be followed when sweeping with sawdust?
    A. Soak, drain, and spread
    B. Spread, drain, and soak
    C. Spread, soak, and drain
    D. Drain, spread, and soak

21. Of the following, it is MOST correct to soak the sawdust in a bucket of water for _____ hour(s).
    A. a half-hour to an
    B. one to two
    C. two to three
    D. three to four

22. The water should be drained from the bucket of sawdust so that excess water does NOT
    A. cause passengers to lose their footing
    B. stain the concrete
    C. flood the tracks
    D. slow down the sweeping

23. Sawdust is dampened in order to
    A. assure good footing on stairways
    B. prevent the raising of dust when sweeping
    C. prevent the staining of concrete
    D. cool off platforms

24. The dampened sawdust may be spread on
    A. wet floors   B. drains   C. stairways   D. mezzanines

Questions 25-27.

DIRECTIONS: Questions 25 through 27 are to be answered SOLELY on the basis of the information contained in the following passage.

Whether a main lobby or upper corridor requires scrubbing or mopping and whether it should be done nightly or less frequently depends on the nature of the floor surface and the amount of traffic. In a building with heavy traffic, it may be desirable every night to scrub the main lobby and to mop the upper floor corridors. In such cases, it may also be found desirable to scrub the upper floors once a week. If traffic is light, it may be only necessary to mop the main lobby every other night and to mop the upper floor corridors once a week. If there is any traffic or usage at all, it will be necessary to at least sweep the corridors nightly.

25. According to the above passage, in a building with light traffic, the upper floor corridors should be
    A. swept every other night
    B. mopped every night
    C. swept nightly
    D. mopped every other night

26. According to the above passage, the number of times a floor is cleaned depends
    A. mainly on the type of floor surface
    B. mainly on the type of traffic
    C. only on the amount of traffic
    D. on both the floor surface and amount of traffic

27. According to the above passage, it may be DESIRABLE to have a heavily used main lobby swept
    A. daily and scrubbed weekly
    B. daily and mopped weekly
    C. and mopped weekly
    D. and scrubbed daily

Questions 28-30.

DIRECTIONS: Questions 28 through 30 are to be answered SOLELY on the basis of the information contained in the following passage.

SENIOR CITIZEN AND HANDICAPPED PASSSENGER REDUCED FARE PROGRAM

Upon display of his or her Medicare Card, Senior Citizen Reduced Fare Card, or Handicapped Photo I.D. Card to the Railroad Clerk on duty, and upon purchase of a token or evidence of having a token, a passenger will be issued a free return trip ticket. The passenger will then be directed to deposit full fare in a turnstile and enter the controlled area. Return trip tickets are valid 24 hours a day, 7 days a week, for the day of purchase and the following two (2) calendar days.

Each return trip ticket will be stamped with the station name and the date only at the time of issuing to a properly identified senior citizen or handicapped passenger. Overstamping of tickets is not allowed. Return trip tickets issued from 2300 hours will be stamped with the date of the following day.

On the return trip, the Railroad Clerk on duty will direct the passenger to enter the controlled area via the exit gate upon the passenger turning in the return trip ticket and displaying his/her Medicare Card, Senior Citizen Reduced Fare Card, or Handicapped Photo I.D. Card.

28. A Railroad Clerk issued a free return ticket to a senior citizen who displayed a birth certificate and a token. The Railroad Clerk's action was
    A. *proper*, because the Railroad Clerk had proof of the senior citizen's age
    B. *improper*, because the senior citizen did not display a Medicare Card, Senior Citizen Reduced Fair Card, or Handicapped Photo I.D. Card
    C. *proper*, because it is inconvenient for many senior citizens to obtain a Medicare Card, Senior Citizen Reduced Fare Card, or Handicapped Photo I.D. Card
    D. *improper*, because the senior citizen did not buy a token from the Railroad Clerk

29. The return trip ticket issued to a senior citizen is valid for ONLY
    A. 24 hours
    B. the day of purchase
    C. two days
    D. the day of purchase and the following two calendar days

30. A Railroad Clerk denied entry to the controlled area via the exit gate to an 18 year-old handicapped passenger who turned in a correctly stamped return trip ticket, but did not display any type of identification card.
    The Railroad Clerk's action was
    A. *proper*, because the passenger should have displayed his Handicapped Photo I.D. Card
    B. *improper*, because the passenger turned in a correctly stamped return trip ticket
    C. *proper*, because the passenger should have displayed either his Handicapped Photo I.D. Card or Social Security Card
    D. *improper*, because it should have been obvious to the Railroad Clerk that the passenger was handicapped

KEY (CORRECT ANSWERS)

1.	C	11.	D	21.	C
2.	C	12.	C	22.	B
3.	B	13.	C	23.	B
4.	B	14.	C	24.	D
5.	B	15.	A	25.	C
6.	A	16.	B	26.	D
7.	A	17.	B	27.	D
8.	A	18.	A	28.	B
9.	C	19.	C	29.	D
10.	B	20.	A	30.	A

TEST 2

DIRECTIONS: Each question or incomplete statement is followed by several suggested answers or completions. Select the one that BEST answers the question or completes the statement. *PRINT THE LETTER OF THE CORRECT ANSWER IN THE SPACE AT THE RIGHT.*

Questions 1-2.

DIRECTIONS: Questions 1 and 2 are to be answered SOLELY on the basis of the information contained in the following passage.

The Commissioner of Investigation shall have general responsibility for the investigation and elimination of corrupt or other criminal activity, conflicts of interest, unethical conduct, misconduct, and incompetence by city agencies, by city officers and employees, and by persons regulated by, doing business with, or receiving funds directly or indirectly from the city, with respect to their dealings with the city. All agency heads shall be responsible for establishing, subject to review for completeness and inter-agency consistency by the Commissioner of Investigation, written standards of conduct for the officials and employees of their respective agencies, and fair and efficient disciplinary systems to maintain those standards of conduct. All agencies shall have an Inspector General who shall report directly to the respective agency head and to the Commissioner of Investigation and be responsible for maintaining standards of conduct as may be established in such agency under this Order. Inspectors General shall be responsible for the investigation and elimination of corrupt or other criminal activity, conflicts of interest, unethical conduct, misconduct, and incompetence within their respective agencies. Except to the extent otherwise provided by law, the employment or continued employment of all existing and prospective Inspectors General and members of their staffs shall be subject to complete background investigations and approval by the Department of Investigation.

1. According to the above passage, establishing written standards of conduct for each agency is the responsibility of the 1.____
   A. agency head
   B. Commissioner of Investigation
   C. Department of Investigation
   D. Inspector General

2. According to the above passage, maintaining standards of conduct within each agency is the responsibility of the 2.____
   A. agency head
   B. Commissioner of Investigation
   C. Department of Investigation
   D. Inspector General

Questions 3-6.

DIRECTIONS: Questions 3 through 6 are to be answered SOLELY on the basis of the information contained in the following passage.

Assume that Warehouse X uses the following procedures for receiving stock. When a delivery is received, the stock handler who receives the delivery should immediately unpack and check the delivery. This check is to ensure that the quantity and kinds of stock items delivered match those on the purchase order which had been sent to the vendor. After the delivery is check, a receiving report is prepared by the same stock handler. This receiving report should include the name of the shipper, the purchase order number, the description of the item, and the actual count or weight of the item. The receiving report, along with the packing slip, should then be checked by the stores clerk against the purchase order to make sure that the quantity received is correct. This is necessary before credit can be obtained from the vendor for any items that are missing or damaged. After the checking is completed, the stock items can be moved to the stockroom.

3. According to the procedures described above, the stock person who receives the delivery should
   A. place the unopened delivery in a secure area for checking at a later date
   B. notify the stores clerk that the delivery has arrived and is ready for checking
   C. unpack the delivery and check the quantity and types of stock items against the purchase order
   D. closely examine the outside of the delivery containers for dents and damages

3.____

4. According to the procedures described above, credit can be obtained from the vendor
   A. *before* the stock handler checks the delivery of stock items
   B. *after* the stock handler checks the delivery of stock items
   C. *before* the stores clerk checks the receiving report against the purchase order
   D. *after* the stores clerk checks the receiving report against the purchase order

4.____

5. According to the procedures described above, all of the following information should be included when filling out a receiving report EXCEPT the
   A. purchase order number   B. name of the shipper
   C. count or weight of the item   D. unit cost per item

5.____

6. According to the procedures described above, after the stores clerk has checked the receiving report against the purchase order, the NEXT step is to
   A. move the stock items to the stockroom
   B. return the stock items received to the vendor
   C. give the stock items to the stock handler for final checking
   D. file the packing slip for inventory purposes

6.____

Questions 7-9.

DIRECTIONS: Questions 7 through 9 are to be answered SOLELY on the basis of the information contained in the following passage.

A filing system for requisition forms used in a warehouse will be of maximum benefit only if it provides ready access to information needed and is not too complex. How effective the system will be depends largely on how well the filing system is organized. A well-organized system usually results in a smooth-running operation.

When setting up a system for filing requisition forms, one effective method would be to first make an alphabetical listing of all the authorized requisitioning agencies. Then file folders should be prepared for each of these agencies and arranged alphabetically in file cabinets. Following this, each agency should be assigned a series of numbers corresponding to those on the blank requisition forms with which they will be supplied. When an agency then submits a requisition and it is filled, the form should be filed in numerical order in the designated agency folder. By using this system, any individual requisition form which is missing from its folder can be easily detected. Regardless of the filing system used, simplicity is essential if the filing system is to be successful.

7. According to the above passage, a filing system is MOST likely to be successful if it is
   A. alphabetical
   B. uncomplicated
   C. numerical
   D. reliable

8. According to the above passage, the reason numbers are assigned to each agency is to
   A. simplify stock issuing procedures
   B. keep a count of all incoming requisition forms
   C. be able to know when a form is missing from its folder
   D. eliminate the need for an alphabetical filing system

9. According to the above passage, which one of the following is an ACCURATE statement regarding the establishment of a well-organized filing system?
   A. Requisitioned stock items will be issued at a faster rate.
   B. Stock items will be stored in storage areas alphabetically arranged.
   C. Information concerning ordered stock items will be easily obtainable.
   D. Maximum productivity can be expected from each employee.

Questions 10-13.

DIRECTIONS: Questions 10 through 13 are to be answered SOLELY on the basis of the information contained in the following passage.

On Tuesday, October 21, Protection Agent Williams, on duty at the Jamaica Depot, observed a man jump over the fence and into the parking lot at 2:12 P.M. and run to a car that was parked with the engine running. The man, who limped slightly, opened the car door, jumped into the car, and sped out of the yard. The car was a 2018 gray Buick Electra, license plate 563-JYN, with parking decal No. 6043. The man was white, about 6 feet tall, about 175 pounds, in his mid-20's, with a scar on his left cheek. He wore a blue sportcoat, tan slacks, a white shift open at the neck with no tie, and brown loafers.

10. What was the color of the car?
    A. White
    B. Blue
    C. Two-tone brown and tan
    D. Gray

11. What were the distinguishing personal features of the man who jumped over   11.____
    the fence?
    A. A scar on the left cheek   B. Pockmarks on his face
    C. A cast on his left wrist   D. Bushy eyebrows

12. What was the number on the car's parking decal?   12.____
    A. 2018   B. 673-JYN   C. 6043   D. 175

13. On what day of the week did the incident occur?   13.____
    A. Monday   B. Tuesday   C. Wednesday   D. Sunday

14. *It is a violation of rules for a Protection Agent to carry a firearm while on*   14.____
    Transit Authority property. The possession of such a weapon, whether carried
    on the person, in a personal vehicle, or stored in a locker, can result in charges
    being filed against the Agent.
    According to the above information, the carrying of a firearm
    A. on Authority property by any employee is prohibited
    B. anywhere by an Agent is prohibited under all circumstances
    C. on Authority property by an Agent is prohibited under all circumstances
    D. anywhere by an Authority employee may be reason for charges being
       filed against that employee

15. *News reporters may enter Authority property if they have the written*   15.____
    authorization of a Public Affairs Department official. The Agent on duty must
    get permission from the Property Protection Control Desk before admitting to
    the property a news person who has no such written authorization.
    If a reporter tells a Protection Agent that she has received permission from the
    Authority President to enter the property, what is the FIRST thing the Agent
    should do?
    A. Call the Authority police.
    B. Admit the reporter immediately.
    C. Call the Authority President's office.
    D. Call the Property Protection Control Desk.

Questions 16-20.

DIRECTIONS: Questions 16 through 20 are to be answered SOLELY on the basis of the
              information contained in the following passage.

<u>FIRES AND EXTINGUISHERS</u>

There are four classes of fires.

Trash fires, paper fires, cloth fires, wood fires, etc. are classified as Class A fires. Water or a water-base solution should be used to extinguish Class A fires. They also can be extinguished by covering the combustibles with a multi-purpose dry chemical.

Burning liquids, gasoline, oil, paint, tar, etc. are considered Class B fires. Such fires can be extinguished by smothering or blanketing them. Extinguishers used for Class B fires are Halon, CO_2, or multi-purpose dry chemical. Water tends to spread such fires and should not be used.

Fires in electrical equipment and switchboards are classified as Class C fires. When live electrical equipment is involved, a non-conducting extinguishing agent like CO_2, a multi-purpose dry chemical, or Halon should always be used. Soda-acid or other water-type extinguishers should not be used.

Class D fires consist of burning metals in finely-divided forms like chips, turnings, and shavings. Specially-designed extinguishing agents that provide a smothering blanket or coating should be used to extinguish Class D fires. Multi-purpose dry-powder extinguishants are such agents.

16. The ONLY type of extinguishing agent that can be used on any type of fire is
    A. a multi-purpose, dry-chemical extinguishing agent
    B. soda-acid
    C. water
    D. carbon dioxide

17. A fire in litter swept from a subway car in a yard is MOST likely to be a Class _____ fire.
    A. A   B. B   C. C   D. D

18. Fire coming from the underbody of a subway car is MOST likely to be a Class _____ fire.
    A. A   B. B   C. C   D. D

19. Which of the following extinguishing agents should NOT be used in fighting a Class C fire involving live electrical equipment?
    A. Halon
    B. Carbon dioxide
    C. A multi-purpose dry chemical
    D. Soda-acid

20. Water is NOT recommended for use on Class B fires because water
    A. would cool the fire
    B. evaporates too quickly
    C. might spread the fire
    D. would smother the fire

Questions 21-24.

DIRECTIONS: Questions 21 through 24 are to be answered SOLELY on the basis of the information contained in the following passage.

Protection Agent Brown, working the midnight to 8:00 A.M. tour at the Flushing Bus Depot, discovered a fire at 2:17 A.M. in Bus No. 4651, which was parked in the southeast portion of the depot yard. He turned in an alarm to the Fire Department from Box 3297 on the nearby street at 2:18 A.M. At 2:20 A.M., he called the Property Protection Control Desk and reported the fire and his action to Line Supervisor Wilson. Line Supervisor Wilson instructed Agent Brown to lock his booth and go to the fire alarm box to direct the fire companies. The first arriving companies were Engine 307 and Ladder 154. Brown directed them to the burning bus. Two minutes later, at 2:23 A.M. Battalion Chief Welsh arrived from Battalion 14. The fire had made little headway. It was extinguished in about two minutes. Brown then wrote a fire report for submittal to Line Supervisor Wilson.

21. What was the FIRST thing Protection Agent Brown did after observing the fire? 21.____
 He
 A. called Battalion Chief Welsh
 B. called the Fire Dispatcher
 C. transmitted an alarm from a nearby alarm box
 D. called 911

22. In what part of the yard was the burning bus? 22.____
 A. Northeast section B. Southwest end
 C. Northwest part D. Southeast portion

23. What time did Agent Brown call Line Supervisor Wilson? 23.____
 A. 2:18 P.M. B. 2:20 A.M. C. 2:29 A.M. D. 2:36 A.M.

24. Which of the following CORRECTLY describes the sequence of Agent Brown's actions? 24.____
 He
 A. saw the fire, turned in an alarm, called the Property Protection Control Desk, directed the fire companies to the fire, and wrote a report
 B. called the Property Protection Control Desk, directed the fire apparatus, directed Chief Welsh, and wrote a report
 C. called Line Supervisor Wilson, turned in an alarm, waited by the burning bus, and directed the fire companies
 D. called Line Supervisor Wilson, directed the firefighters, waited for instructions from Line Supervisor Wilson, and wrote a report

Questions 25-26.

DIRECTIONS: Questions 25 and 26 are to be answered SOLELY on the basis of the information contained in the following passage.

Protection Agents may admit to Transit Authority headquarters only persons with Transit Authority passes, persons with job appointment letters, and persons who have permission to enter from Transit Authority officials.

During his tour in the Authority's headquarters lobby, Protection Agent Williams admitted to the building 326 persons with Authority passes and 41 persons with job appointment letters. He telephoned authorized officials for permission to admit 14 others, 13 of whom were granted permission and entered and one of whom was denied permission. He also turned away two persons who wanted to enter to sell to employees merchandise for their personal use, and one person who appeared inebriated.

25. How many persons did Agent Williams admit to the building? 25.____
 A. 326 B. 367 C. 380 D. 382

26. To how many persons did Agent Williams refuse admittance? 26.____
 A. 4 B. 13 C. 14 D. 41

Questions 27-30.

DIRECTIONS: Questions 27 through 30 are to be answered SOLELY on the basis of the information contained in the following instructions on Lost Property.

LOST PROPERTY

All inquiries for information regarding lost property will be referred to the Lost Property Office. Any Station Department employee finding a lost article, of any description, will immediately hand it over to the railroad clerk in the nearest 24-hour booth of the station where the article is found. The clerk must give the employee a receipt for the article. Should a passenger hand over a lost article to a cleaner, the cleaner will offer to escort the passenger to the nearest 24-hour booth in order that a receipt may be given by the railroad clerk there. If the passenger declines, the cleaner will accept the lost article without giving a receipt and proceed as desired above. Each employee who receive lost property will be held responsible for it unless he produces a receipt for it from another employee. Should any lost property disappear, the last employee who signed for it will be held accountable.

27. If a cleaner turns in a lost article to a railroad clerk in the nearest 24-hour booth, 27.____
 he should make sure that he
 A. gets a receipt for the article
 B. notifies his supervisor about the lost article
 C. finds out the name of the owner of the article
 D. writes a report on the incident

28. If a lost article disappears after a cleaner has properly turned it in to the 28.____
 railroad clerk in the nearest 24-hour booth, the one who will be held
 accountable is the
 A. person who found the lost article
 B. cleaner who turned in the article
 C. supervisor in charge of the station
 D. last employee to sign a receipt for the article

29. A passenger finds a lost article and gives it to a cleaner. The cleaner gives the 29.____
 passenger a receipt.
 The cleaner's action was
 A. *proper*, because the passenger was relieved of any responsibility for the lost article
 B. *improper*, because the cleaner should have offered to escort the passenger to the nearest 24-hour booth
 C. *proper*, because the cleaner is required to give the passenger a receipt
 D. *improper*, because the cleaner should have sent the passenger to the Lost Property Office

30. A cleaner finds a five dollar bill on a crowded station platform. Three passengers who see him pick it up rush up and claim the money. The first passenger said he had just taken a roll of bills out of his pocket and must have dropped it. The second said he had just given two five dollar bills to his wife, and she had dropped one of them. The third said he had a hole in his pocket and the bill fell out of it.
The cleaner should
   A. give the five dollar bill t the second passenger because he had his wife as a witness
   B. give the five dollar bill to the third passenger because he had a hole in his pocket
   C. keep the five dollar bill
   D. bring the five dollar bill to the railroad clerk in the nearest 24-hour booth

30.____

KEY (CORRECT ANSWERS)

1.	A	11.	A	21.	C
2.	D	12.	C	22.	D
3.	C	13.	B	23.	B
4.	D	14.	C	24.	A
5.	D	15.	D	25.	C
6.	A	16.	A	26.	A
7.	B	17.	A	27.	A
8.	C	18.	C	28.	D
9.	C	19.	D	29.	B
10.	D	20.	C	30.	D

ARITHMETICAL REASONING
EXAMINATION SECTION
TEST 1

DIRECTIONS: Each question or incomplete statement is followed by several suggested answers or completions. Select the one that BEST answers the question or completes the statement. *PRINT THE LETTER OF THE CORRECT ANSWER IN THE SPACE AT THE RIGHT.*

1. Assume that it takes approximately 1 1/2 minutes to unload a dozen identical items from a delivery truck.
   At this speed, the amount of time it should take to unload a shipment of 876 items is, MOST NEARLY, _____ minutes.
   A. 90   B. 100   C. 110   D. 120

   1.____

2. Assume that a shop clerk has received a bill of $108 for a delivery of clamps which cost $4.32 per dozen.
   How many clamps should there be in this delivery?
   A. 25   B. 36   C. 300   D. 360

   2.____

3. Employee A has not used any leave time and has accumulated a total of 45 leave-days.
   How many months did it take employee A to have accumulated 45 leave-days if the accrual rate is 1 2/3 days per months?
   A. 25   B. 27   C. 29   D. 31

   3.____

4. A shop clerk is notified that only 75 bolts can be supplied by Vendor A.
   If this represents 12.5% of the total requisition, then how many bolts were originally ordered?
   A. 125   B. 600   C. 700   D. 900

   4.____

5. An enclosed square-shaped storage area with sides of 16 feet each has a safe-load capacity of 250 pounds per square foot.
   The MAXIMUM evenly distributed weight that can be stored in this area is _____ lbs.
   A. 1,056   B. 4,000   C. 64,000   D. 102,400

   5.____

6. A clerical employee completed 70 progress reports the first week, 87 the second week, and 80 the third week.
   Assuming a 4-week month, how many progress reports must the clerk complete in the fourth week in order to attain an average of 85 progress reports per week for the month?
   A. 93   B. 103   C. 113   D. 133

   6.____

2 (#1)

7. On the first of the month, Shop X received a delivery of 150 gallons of lubricating oil. During the month, the following amounts of oil were used on lubricating work each week: 30 quarts, 36 quarts, 20 quarts, and 48 quarts.
The amount of lubricating oil remaining at the end of the month was _____ gallons.
   A. 4 B. 33.5 C. 41.5 D. 116.5

7._____

8. For working a 35-hour week, Employee A earns a gross amount of $160.30. For each hour that Employee A works over 40 hours a week, he is entitled to 1 1/2 times his hourly wage rate.
If Employee A worked 9 hours on Monday, 8 hours on Tuesday, 9 hours 30 minutes on Wednesday, 9 hours 15 minutes on Thursday, and 9 hours 15 minutes on Friday, what should his gross salary be for that week?
   A. $206.10 B. $210.68 C. $217.55 D. $229.00

8._____

9. An enclosed cube-shaped storage bay has dimensions of 12 feet by 12 feet by 12 feet. Standard procedure requires that there be at least 1 foot of space between the walls, the ceiling and the stored items.
What is the MAXIMUM number of cube-shaped boxes with length, width, and height of 1 foot each that can be stored on 1-foot high pallets in this bay?
   A. 1,000 B. 1,331 C. 1,452 D. 1,728

9._____

10. Assume that two ceilings are to be painted. One ceiling measures 30 feet by 15 feet and the second 45 feet by 60 feet.
If one quart of paint will cover 60 square feet of ceiling, approximately how much paint will be required to paint the two ceilings?
   A. 6 gallons B. 10 gallons C. 13 gallons D. 18 gallons

10._____

KEY (CORRECT ANSWERS)

1.	C	6.	B
2.	C	7.	D
3.	B	8.	C
4.	B	9.	A
5.	C	10.	C

3 (#1)

SOLUTIONS TO PROBLEMS

1. 876 ÷ 12 = 73. Then, (73)(1 1/2) = 109.5 ≈ 110 minutes.

2. $108 ÷ $4.32 = 25. Then, (25)(12) = 300 clamps.

3. 45 ÷ 1 1/2 = 27 months

4. 75 ÷ .125 = 600 bolts

5. (16)(16)(250) == 64,000 pounds

6. (85)(4) = 340. Then, 340 – 70 – 87 – 80 = 103 progress reports.

7. Changing every calculation to gallons, the amount of oil remaining is 150 – 7.5 – 9 – 5 – 12 = 116.5.

8. 9 + 8 + 9.5 + 9.25 + 9.25 = 45 hours. His gross pay will be ($4.58)(40) + ($6.87)(5) = $217.55. (Note: To get his regular hourly wages, divide $160.30 by 35.)

9. 12 – 1 – 1 =10. Maximum number of boxes is $(10)^3$ = 1000.

10. First ceiling contains (30)(15) = 450 sq.ft., whereas the second ceiling contains (45)(60) = 2700 sq.ft. The total sq.ft. = 3150. Now, 3150 ÷ 60 = 52.5 quarts of paint = 13.125 or 13 gallons.

TEST 2

DIRECTIONS: Each question or incomplete statement is followed by several suggested answers or completions. Select the one that BEST answers the question or completes the statement. *PRINT THE LETTER OF THE CORRECT ANSWER IN THE SPACE AT THE RIGHT.*

1. A piping sketch is drawn to a scale of 1/8" = 1 foot.
   A vertical steam line measuring 3/4" on the sketch would have an actual length of _____ feet.
   A. 16   B. 22   C. 24   D. 28

   1._____

2. Three lengths of pipe 1'10", 3'2 1/2", and 5'7 1/2", respectively, are to be cut from a pipe 14'0" long.
   Allowing 1/8" for each pipe cut, the length of pipe remaining is
   A. 3'1 1/8"   B. 3'2 1/2"   C. 3'3 1/2"   D. 3'3 5/8"

   2._____

3. Assume that a steamfitter's helper earns $11.16 an hour and that he works 250 seven-hour days a year.
   His gross yearly salary will be
   A. 19,430   B. $19,530   C. $19,650   D. $19,780

   3._____

4. A pipe having an inside diameter of 3.48 inches and a wall thickness of .18 inches, will have an outside diameter of _____ inches.
   A. 3.84   B. 3.64   C. 3.57   D. 3.51

   4._____

5. A rectangular steel bar having a volume of 30 cubic inches, a width of 2 inches, and a height of 3 inches will have a length of _____ inches.
   A. 12   B. 10   C. 8   D. 5

   5._____

6. A pipe weighs 20.4 pounds per foot of length.
   The total weight of eight pieces of this pipe with each piece 20 feet in length is MOST NEARLY _____ pounds.
   A. 460   B. 1680   C. 2420   D. 3260

   6._____

7. In last year's budget, $7,500 was spent for office supplies. Of this amount, 60% was spent for paper supplies.
   If the price of paper has risen 20% over last year's price, then the amount that will be spent this year on paper supplies, assuming the same quantity will be purchased, will be
   A. $3,600   B. $5,200   C. $5,400   D. $6,000

   7._____

8. If it takes 4 painters 54 days to do a certain paint job, then the time it should take 5 painters working at the same speed to do the same job is MOST NEARLY _____ days.
   A. 3 1/2   B. 4   C. 4 1/2   D. 5

   8._____

9. A foreman assigns a gang foreman to supervise a job which must be completed at the end of 7 working days. The gang foreman has 8 maintainers in his gang. At the end of 3 working days, although the work has been efficiently done, the job is only one-third completed.
   In order to complete the job on time, without overtime, the gang foreman should request that he be given _____ more maintainers.
   A. 3   B. 4   C. 5   D. 6

10. One shipment of 70 shovels costs $140. A second shipment of 130 shovels costs $208.00.
    The average cost per shovel for both shipments is MOST NEARLY
    A. $1.60   B. $1.75   C. $2.00   D. $2.50

KEY (CORRECT ANSWERS)

1.	D	6.	D
2.	D	7.	C
3.	B	8.	C
4.	A	9.	B
5.	D	10.	B

SOLUTIONS TO PROBLEMS

1. 3 1/2 ÷ 1/8 = 28 feet.

2. 14' − 1'10" − 3' 1/2" − 5'7 1/2" − 1/8" − 1/8" − 1/8" = 3'3 5/8"

3. (250(7) = 1750 hours. Then, ($11.16)(1750) = $19,530

4. Outside diameter = 3.48 + .18 + .18 = 3.84 inches

5. Length is 30 ÷ 2 ÷ 3 = 5 inches

6. (20)(8) = 160 feet. Then, (160)(20.4) = 3264 ≈ 3260 pounds

7. ($7,500)(.60) = $4,500. Then, ($4,500)(1.20) = $5,400

8. Let x = required days. Since this is an inverse ratio, 4/5 = x/5 1/2. Then, 5x = 22.
   Solving, x = 4.4 ≈ 4 1/2

9. (8)(3) = 24 man-days were needed to complete 1/3 of the job.
   Since 2/3 of the job remains, the foreman will need 48 man-days for the remaining 4 days.
   This requires 12 men. Since he has 8 currently, he will need 4 more workers.

10. Average cost per shovel is ($140 + $208) ÷ (70+130) = $1.74, which is closest to $1.75.

TEST 3

DIRECTIONS: Each question or incomplete statement is followed by several suggested answers or completions. Select the one that BEST answers the question or completes the statement. *PRINT THE LETTER OF THE CORRECT ANSWER IN THE SPACE AT THE RIGHT.*

1. Assume that your warehouse received a shipment of 600 articles. A sample of 60 articles was inspected. Of this sample, one article was wholly defective and four articles were partly defective.
   On the basis of this sampling, you would expect the total number of defective articles in this shipment to be
   A. 5   B. 10   C. 40   D. 50

   1.____

2. Assume that you have been instructed to order mineral spirits as soon as the supply-on-hand falls to the level required for sixty days of issue.
   If the total amount of mineral spirits on hand is 960 gallons and you issue an average of 8 gallons of mineral spirits per day, and your warehouse works a five-day week, you will be required to order mineral spirits in _____ working days.
   A. 50   B. 60   C. 70   D. 80

   2.____

3. Assume that you work in a one-story warehouse where the total available floor space measures 175 feet by 140 feet. Of this floor space, one area measuring 35 feet by 75 feet is used for storing materials handling equipment, another area is measuring 10 feet by 21 feet is used for office space, and the remaining floor space is available for storage.
   The amount of floor space available for storage in this one-story warehouse is _____ square feet.
   A. 21,665   B. 21,875   C. 24,290   D. $24,500

   3.____

4. Assume that linoleum tiles measuring 9 inches by 9 inches are packed ten to a box and each box costs $3.50.
   The cost of buying enough linoleum tiles to cover an area measuring 15 feet by 21 feet is
   A. $98.00   B. $110.25   C. $196.00   D. $220.50

   4.____

5. The number of boxes measuring 3 inches by 3 inches by 3 inches that will fit into a carton measuring 2 feet by 4 feet is
   A. 2,048   B. 2,645   C. 7,936   D. 23,808

   5.____

6. The stock inventory card for paint, white, flat, one-gallon, has the following entries:

Date	Received	Shipped	Balance
April 12	-	25	75
April 13	50	75	
April 14	-	10	
April 15	25		
April 16			

   6.____

2 (#3)

The balance on hand at the close of business on April 15 should be
A. 40 B. 45 C. 55 D. 65

7. The cost of one dozen pieces of screening, each measuring 4 feet 6 inches at $.10 per square foot is
A. $22.50 B. $25.00 C. $27.00 D. $27.60

8. Assume that it takes an average of ten man-hours to stack four tons of a particular item.
In order to stack 80 tons, the number of men required to complete the job in twenty hours is
A. 10 B. 20 C. 30 D. 40

9. Assume that you are required to relocate 5,000 reams of unboxed paper using only manual labor. The average time required for one laborer to pick 12 reams, carry them to the new location, and store them properly is ten minutes.
In order to complete this relocation task within one working day of seven hours, the MINIMUM number of laborers you should assign to this task is
A. 10 B. 15 C. 24 D. 70

10. Assume that you receive a shipment of 9 boxes of paper towels. Each box contains 6 dozen packages. Each package contains 200 paper towels. The total cost of the shipment of boxes is $64.80. The unit of issue for paper towels is the package.
The unit cost of the paper towels is
A. $.10 B. $.90 C. $1.20 D. $7.20

KEY (CORRECT ANSWERS)

1. D   6. D
2. B   7. C
3. A   8. A
4. C   9. A
5. A   10. A

SOLUTIONS TO PROBLEMS

1. Solve for x: 5/60 = x/600. Then, x = 50

2. 960 ÷ 8 = 120 days. Then, 120 – 60 = 60 days

3. Storage area is (175)(140) – (35)(75) – (10)(21) = 21,665 sq.ft.

4. 9 × 9 = 81 sq.in. (81)(10) = 810 sq.in. of tiles cost $3.50. (15ft)(21ft) = (180)(252) = 45,360 sq.in. Now, 45,360 ÷ 810 = 56 boxes. Finally, (56)($3.50) = $196

5. (2ft)(4ft)(4ft) = (24 in)(48 in)(48 in) = 55,296 sq.in. Then, 55,296/27 = 2048 boxes.

6. Balance at end of April 13th is 75 + 50 – 75 = 50
Balance at end of April 14th is 50 + 0 – 10 = 40
Balance at end of April 15th is 40 + 25 – 0 = 65

7. (4 1/2)(5) = 224 sq.ft. Then, (22)($0.10) = $2.25 per piece. The cost of 12 pieces is ($2.25)(12) = $27

8. If 10 man-hours are needed for 4 tons, then 200 man-hours are needed for 80 tons. The number of men needed to do the job in 20 hours is 200 ÷ 20 = 10

9. 7 hours = 420 minutes and 420 ÷ 10 = 42.
Then, (42)(12) = 504 reams transported per day for each laborer. Now, 5000 ÷ 504 ≈ 9.92, which gets rounded up to 10.

10. (9)(72) = 648 package. Then, $64.80 ÷ 648 = $0.10

NAME AND NUMBER CHECKING
EXAMINATION SECTION
TEST 1

DIRECTIONS: This test is designed to measure your speed/and accuracy. You are urged to work both quickly and accurately and to do correctly as many lists as you can in the time allowed. The test consists of lists or pairs of names and numbers. Count the number of IDENTICAL pairs in each list. Then, select the correct number, 1, 2, 3, 4, 5, and indicate your choice in the space at the right. Two sample questions are presented for your guidance, together with the correct solutions.

SAMPLE LIST A
Adelphi College — Adelphia College
Braxton Corp — Braxeton Corp.
Wassaic State School — Wassaic State School
Central Islip State Hospital — Central Isllip State Hospital
Greenwich House — Greenwich House

NOTE: There are only two correct pairs—Wassaic State School and Greenwich House. Therefore, the CORRECT answer is 2.

SAMPLE LIST B
78453694 — 78453684
784530 — 784530
533 — 534
67845 — 67845
2368745 — 2368755

NOTE: There are only two correct pairs—784530 and 67845. Therefore, the CORRECT answer is 2.

LIST 1   1.____
   98654327   - 98654327
   74932564   - 7492564
   61438652   - 61438652
   01297653   - 01287653
   1865439765   - 1865439765

LIST 2   2.____
   478362   - 478363
   278354792   - 278354772
   9327   - 9327
   297384625   - 27384625
   6428156   - 6428158

2 (#1)

LIST 3   3._____
    Abbey House — Abbey House
    Actor's Fund Home — Actor's Fund Home
    Adrian Memorial — Adrian Memorial
    A. Clayton Powell Home — Clayton Powell House
    Abbot E. Kittredge Club — Abbott E. Kitteredge Club

LIST 4   4._____
    3682 — 3692
    21937453829 — 31927453829
    723 — 733
    2763920 — 2763920
    47293 — 47293

LIST 5   5._____
    Adra House — Adra House
    Adolescents' Court — Adolescents' Court
    Cliff Villa — Cliff Villa
    Clark Neighborhood House — Clark Neighborhood House
    Alma Mathews House — Alma Mathews House

LIST 6   6._____
    28734291 — 28734271
    63810263849 — 63810263846
    26831027 — 26831027
    368291 — 368291
    7238102637 — 7238102637

LIST 7   7._____
    Albion State T.S. — Albion State T.C.
    Clara de Hirsch Home — Clara De Hirsch Home
    Alice Carrington Royce — Alice Carington Royce
    Alice Chopin Nursery — Alice Chapin Nursery
    Lighthouse Eye Clinic — Lighthouse Eye Clinic

LIST 8   8._____
    327 — 329
    712438291026 — 712438291026
    2753829142 — 275382942
    826287 — 826289
    26435162839 — 26435162839

LIST 9   9._____
    Letchworth Village — Letchworth Village
    A.A.A.E. Inc. — A.A.A.E. Inc.
    Clear Pool Camp — Clear Pool Camp
    A.M.M.L.A. Inc. — A.M.M.L.A. Inc.
    J.G. Harbard — J.G. Harbord

3 (#1)

LIST 10   10.____
    8254   - 8256
    2641526   - 2641526
    4126389012   - 4126389102
    725   - 725
    76253917287   - 76253917287

LIST 11   11.____
    Attica State Prison   - Attica State Prison
    Nellie Murrah   - Nellie Murrah
    Club Marshall   - Club Marshal
    Assissium Casea-Maria - Assissium Casa-Maria
    The Homestead   - The Homestead

LIST 12   12.____
    2691   - 2691
    623819253627   - 623819253629
    28637   - 28937
    278392736   - 278392736
    52739   - 52739

LIST 13   13.____
    A.I.C.P. Boys Camp   - A.I.C.P. Boy's Camp
    Einar Chrystie   - Einar Christyie
    Astoria Center   - Astoria Center
    G. Frederick Brown   - G. Federick Browne
    Vacation Service   - Vacation Services

LIST 14   14.____
    728352689   - 728352688
    643728   - 643728
    37829176   - 37827196
    8425367   - 8425369
    65382018   - 65382018

LIST 15   15.____
    E.S. Streim   - E.S. Strim
    Charles E. Higgins   - Charles E. Higgins
    Baluvelt, N.Y.   - Blauwelt, N.Y.
    Roberta Magdalen   - Roberto Magdalen
    Ballard School   - Ballard School

LIST 16   16.____
    7382   - 7392
    281374538299   - 291374538299
    623   - 633
    6273730   - 6273730
    63392   - 63392

LIST 17
Orrin Otis — - Orrin Otis
Barat Settlement — - Barat Settlemen
Emmanuel House — - Emmanuel House
William T. McCreery — - William T. McCreery
Seamen's Home — - Seaman's Home

17.____

LIST 18
72824391 — - 72834371
3729106237 — - 37291106237
82620163849 — - 82620163846
37638921 — - 37638921
82631027 — - 82631027

18.____

LIST 19
Commonwealth Fund — - Commonwealth Fund
Anne Johnsen — - Anne Johnson
Bide-A-Wee Home — - Bide-a-Wee Home
Riverdale-on-Hudson — - Riverdal-on-Hudson
Bialystoker Home — - Bailystoker Home

19.____

LIST 20
9271 — - 9271
392918352627 — - 392018852629
72637 — - 72637
927392736 — - 927392736
92739 — - 92739

20.____

LIST 21
Charles M. Stump — - Charles M. Stump
Bourne Workshop — - Buorne Workshop
B'nai Bi'rith — - B'nai Brith
Poppenhuesen Institute — - Poppenheusen Institute
Consular Service — - Consular Service

21.____

LIST 22
927352689 — - 927352688
647382 — - 648382
93729176 — - 93727196
649536718 — - 649536718
5835367 — - 5835369

22.____

LIST 23
L.S. Bestend — - L.S. Bestent
Hirsch Mfg. Co. — - Hircsh Mfg. Co.
F.H. Storrs — - F.P. Storrs
Camp Wassaic — - Camp Wassaic
George Ballingham — - George Ballingham

23.____

5 (#1)

LIST 24   24.____
　　372846392048   - 372846392048
　　334   - 334
　　7283524678   - 7283524678
　　7283   - 7283
　　7283629372   - 7283629372

LIST 25   25.____
　　Dr. Stiles Company   - Dr. Stills Company
　　Frances Hunsdon   - Frances Hunsdon
　　Northrop Barrert   - Nothrup Barrent
　　J.D. Brunjes   - J.D. Brunjes
　　Theo. Claudel & Co.   - Theo. Claudel co.

KEY (CORRECT ANSWERS)

1.	3	11.	3
2.	1	12.	3
3.	2	13.	1
4.	2	14.	2
5.	5	15.	2
6.	3	16.	2
7.	1	17.	3
8.	2	18.	2
9.	4	19.	2
10.	3	20.	4

21.	2
22.	1
23.	2
24.	5
25.	2

TEST 2

DIRECTIONS: This test is designed to measure your speed/and accuracy. You are urged to work both quickly and accurately and to do correctly as many lists as you can in the time allowed. The test consists of lists or pairs of names and numbers. Count the number of IDENTICAL pairs in each list. Then, select the correct number, 1, 2, 3, 4, 5, and indicate your choice in the space at the right.

LIST 1   1._____
    82728   - 82738
    82736292637   - 82736292639
    728   - 738
    83926192527   - 83726192529
    82736272   - 82736272

LIST 2   2._____
    L. Pietri   - L. Pietri
    Mathewson, L.F.   - Mathewson, L.F.
    Funk & Wagnall   - Funk & Wagnalls
    Shimizu, Sojio   - Shimizu, Sojio
    Filing Equipment Bureau   - Filing Equipment Buraeu

LIST 3   3._____
    63801829374   - 63801839474
    283577657   - 283577657
    65689   - 65689
    3457892026   - 3547893026
    2779   - 2778

LIST 4   4._____
    August Caille   - August Caille
    The Well-Fare Service   - The Wel-Fare Service
    K.L.M. Process co.   - R.L.M. Process Co.
    Merrill Littell   - Merrill Littell
    Dodd & Sons   - Dodd & Son

LIST 5   5._____
    998745732   - 998745733
    723   - 723
    463849102983   - 463849102983
    8570   - 8570
    279012   - 279012

LIST 6   6._____
    M.A. Wender   - M.A. Winder
    Minneapolis Supply Co.   - Minneapolis Supply Co.
    Beverly Hills Corp   - Beverley Hills Corp.
    Trafalgar Square   - Trafalgar Square
    Phifer, D.T.   - Phiefer, D.T.

LIST 7
    7834629   - 7834629
    3549806746   - 3549806746
    97802564   - 97892564
    689246   - 688246
    2578024683   - 2578024683

7.____

LIST 8
    Scadrons'   - Scadrons'
    Gensen & Bro.   - Genson & Bro.
    Firestone Co.   - Firestone Co.
    H.L. Eklund   - H.L. Eklund
    Oleomargarine Co.   - Oleomargarine Co.

8.____

LIST 9
    782039485618   - 782039485618
    53829172639   - 63829172639
    892   - 892
    82937482   - 829374820
    52937456   - 53937456

9.____

LIST 10
    First Nat'l Bank   - First Nat'l Bank
    Sedgwick Machine Works   - Sedgewick Machine Works
    Hectographia Co.   - Hectographia Corp.
    Levet Bros.   - Levet Bros.
    Multistamp Co., Inc.   - Multistamp Co., Inc.

10.____

LIST 11
    7293   - 7293
    6382910293   - 6382910292
    981928374012   - 981928374912
    58293   - 58393
    18203649271   - 283019283745

11.____

LIST 12
    Lowrey Lb'r Co.   - Lowrey Lb'r Co.
    Fidelity Service   - Fidelity Service
    Reumann, J.A.   - Reumann, J.A.
    Duophoto Ltd.   - Duophotos Ltd.
    John Jarratt   - John Jaratt

12.____

LIST 13
    6820384   - 6820384
    383019283745   - 383019283745
    63927102   - 63928102
    91029354829   - 91029354829
    58291728   - 58291728

13.____

LIST 14
    Standard Press Co.   - Standard Press Co.
    Reliant Mf'g. Co.   - Relant Mf'g Co.
    M.C. Lynn   - M.C. Lynn
    J. Fredericks Company   - G. Fredericks Company
    Wandermann, B.S.   - Wanderman, B.S.

14.____

LIST 15
    4283910293   - 4283010203
    992018273648   - 992018273848
    620   - 629
    752937273   - 752937373
    5392   - 5392

15.____

LIST 16
    Waldorf Hotel   - Waldorf Hotel
    Aaron Machinery Co.   - Aaron Machinery Co.
    Caroline Ann Locke   - Caroline Ane Locke
    McCabe Mfg. Co.   - McCabe Mfg. Co.
    R.L. Landres   - R.L. Landers

16.____

LIST 17
    68391028364   - 68391028394
    68293   - 68293
    739201   - 739201
    72839201   - 72839211
    739917   - 739719

17.____

LIST 18
    Balsam M.M.   - Balsamm, M.M.
    Steinway & Co.   - Stienway & M. Co.
    Eugene Elliott   - Eugene A. Elliott
    Leonard Loan Co.   - Leonard Loan Co.
    Frederick Morgan   - Frederick Morgen

18.____

LIST 19
    8929   - 9820
    392836472829   - 392836572829
    462   - 4622039271
    827   - 2039276837
    53829   - 54829

19.____

LIST 20
    Danielson's Hofbrau   - Danielson's Hafbrau
    Edward A. Truarme   - Edward A. Truame
    Insulite Co.   - Insulite Co.
    Reisler Shoe Corp.   - Rielser Shoe Corp.
    L.L. Thompson   - L.L. Thompson

20.____

4 (#2)

LIST 21   21.____
   92839102837   - 92839102837
   58891028   - 58891028
   7291728   - 7291928
   272839102839   - 272839102839
   428192   - 428102

LIST 22   22.____
   K.L. Veiller   - K.L. Veiller
   Webster, Roy   - Webster, Ray
   Drasner Spring Co.   - Drasner Spring Co.
   Edward J. Cravenport   - Edward J. Cravanport
   Harold Field   - Harold A. Field

LIST 23   23.____
   2293   - 2293
   4283910293   - 5382910292
   871928374012   - 871928374912
   68293   - 68393
   8120364927   - 81293649271

LIST 24   24.____
   Tappe, Inc   - Tappe, Inc.
   A.M. Wentingworth   - A.M. Wentinworth
   Scott A. Elliott   - Scott A. Elliott
   Echeverria Corp.   - Echeverria Corp.
   Bradford Victor Company - Bradford Victer Company

LIST 25   25.____
   4820384   - 4820384
   393019283745   - 283919283745
   63917102   - 63927102
   91029354829   - 91029354829
   48291728   - 48291728

KEY (CORRECT ANSWERS)

1.	1	11.	1
2.	3	12.	3
3.	2	13.	4
4.	2	14.	2
5.	4	15.	1
6.	2	16.	3
7.	3	17.	2
8.	4	18.	1
9.	2	19.	1
10.	3	20.	2

21.	3
22.	2
23.	1
24.	2
25.	4

INTERPRETING STATISTICAL DATA GRAPHS, CHARTS AND TABLES

EXAMINATION SECTION
TEST 1

DIRECTIONS: Each question or incomplete statement is followed by several suggested answers or completions. Select the one that BEST answers the question or completes the statement. *PRINT THE LETTER OF THE CORRECT ANSWER IN THE SPACE AT THE RIGHT.*

Questions 1-3.

DIRECTIONS: Questions 1 through 3 are to be answered on the basis of the following charts and information.

AREA 1

Section A	Section B
Stationery	Electrical supplies
Office supplies	Lighting equipment
Kitchenware	Dry goods

AREA 2

Section A	Section B
Drugs	Tools
Chemicals	Laboratory equipment
Cleaning supplies	Hospital supplies

The above charts represent a storage room which is separated into two areas, Area 1 and Area 2, and separated within each area into two sections, Section A and Section B. Each section stores the items shown on the charts.

1. According to the above charts, you should find laboratory equipment in Area _____, Section _____. 1.____

   A. 1; A B. 1; B C. 2; A D. 2; B

2. According to the above charts, all of the following items are in Area 1, Section A EXCEPT 2.____

   A. dry goods B. stationery
   C. kitchenware D. office supplies

3. According to the above charts, you should store light bulbs in Area _____, Section _____. 3.____

   A. 1; A B. 1; B C. 2; A D. 2; B

101

2 (#1)

KEY (CORRECT ANSWERS)

1. D
2. A
3. B

TEST 2

Questions 1-3.

DIRECTIONS: Questions 1 through 3 are to be answered on the basis of the information given in the stock listing below.

STOCK LISTING OF BOLTS, NUTS, SCREWS, WASHERS, ETC.

Item No.	Commodity Code	Description
1	43-A00059	Anchor Expansion Mach Screw Type 6/32 inch
2	43-A00061	Anchor Expansion Mach Screw Type 8/32 inch
3	43-B06028	Bolt Carriage Oval HD Hex Nut 3/16 x 1 inch
4	43-B06029	Bolt Carriage Oval HD Hex Nut 3/16 x 1 1/2 inch
5	43-N06033	Nut Mach Screw Brass Hex 4/40 inch
6	43-N04725	Nut Mach Screw Brass Hex 6/40 inch
7	43-S08963	Screw Mach Brass Rnd HD 6/32 x 1 inch
8	43-S08975	Screw Mach Brass Rnd HD 6/32 x 2 inch
9	43-W00700	Washer Brass Round 1 lb. pkg No. 4
10	43-W03024	Washer Brass Round 1 lb. pkg No. 6

1. The type of item which is described as 1 lb. pkg is a

    A. bolt   B. nut   C. screw   D. washer

2. The Commodity Code which appears in the next row below Commodity Code 43-B06029 is

    A. 43-A00061   B. 43-B06028   C. 43-N06033   D. 43-N04725

3. The one of the following which does NOT have the complete information taken from the Description column of the item is

    A. Anchor Expansion Mach Screw Type 8/32 inch
    B. Bolt Carriage Oval Nut 3/16 x 1 1/2 inch
    C. Nut Mach Screw Brass Hex 6/40 inch
    D. Screw Mach Brass Rnd HD 6/32 x 2 inch

KEY (CORRECT ANSWERS)

1. D
2. C
3. B

TEST 3

Questions 1-3.

DIRECTIONS: Questions 1 through 3 are to be answered on the basis of the information given in the chart shown below.

Item	Weight
Metal file box	5 pounds
Large desk stapler	2 pounds
Large tape dispenser	1.5 pounds
Hardcover dictionary	3 pounds

1. Based on the figures shown in the chart above, the TOTAL weight of 5 metal file boxes, 3 hardcover dictionaries, and a large tape dispenser is _____ pounds.

    A. 33.5 B. 34.5 C. 35.5 D. 36.5

2. Of the following, which group of items would weigh a TOTAL of 25 pounds or less?

    A. 6 metal file boxes and 1 hardcover dictionary
    B. 10 large desk staplers and 1 hardcover dictionary
    C. 8 hardcover dictionaries and 2 large tape dispensers
    D. 10 large tape dispensers and 3 metal file boxes

3. Assume that 5 large desk staplers, 6 metal file boxes, 10 hardcover dictionaries, and 3 large tape dispensers are placed in a shipping container with a weight limit of 100 pounds.
    When you add up the total weight of the items, the number of pounds under the weight limit would be _____ pounds.

    A. 23.5 B. 24.5 C. 25.5 D. 26.5

KEY (CORRECT ANSWERS)

1. C
2. B
3. C

TEST 4

Questions 1-5.

DIRECTIONS: Questions 1 through 5 are to be answered on the basis of the information given in the stock listing below.

LISTING OF ENVELOPES IN STOCK

Item No.	Description	Unit of Issue (per carton)	Amount (cartons)
1	Envelope Commercial White 3 5/8" x 6 1/2"	1000	14
2	Envelope Commercial White 4 1/2" x 9 1/2"	2500	7
3	Envelope Open End Metal Clasp 7" x 10"	1000	16
4	Envelope Open End Metal Clasp 8 1/2" x 11 1/2"	1000	15
5	Envelope Open End Metal Clasp 9 1/2" x 12 1/2"	500	28
6	Envelope Open End Metal Clasp 11 1/2" x 14 1/2"	500	24

1. The TOTAL number of cartons of envelopes in stock is

    A. 87 B. 84 C. 100 D. 104

2. The envelopes which all have a unit of issue of 1000 per carton are found in Item Nos.

    A. 1, 2, and 3 B. 1, 3, and 4
    C. 2, 4, and 5 D. 3, 4, and 6

3. The item for which there is the GREATEST number of envelopes in stock is Item No.

    A. 2 B. 3 C. 4 D. 5

4. The TOTAL number of envelopes in stock for all of the items listed above is

    A. 74,000 B. 81,000 C. 88,500 D. 104,500

5. You receive an order for the following items: Item No. 1, 2000 envelopes; Item No. 2, 5000 envelopes; Item No. 4, 2000 envelopes; Item No. 6, 1000 envelopes. The TOTAL number of cartons that you will have to pick from stock in filling the order is

    A. 6 B. 7 C. 8 D. 9

KEY (CORRECT ANSWERS)

1. D
2. B
3. A
4. C
5. C

TEST 5

DIRECTIONS: Each question or incomplete statement is followed by several suggested answers or completions. Select the one that BEST answers the question or completes the statement. *PRINT THE LETTER OF THE CORRECT ANSWER IN THE SPACE AT THE RIGHT.*

Questions 1-5.

DIRECTIONS: Questions 1 through 5 are to be answered on the basis of the information given in Tables 1 and 2 of the DAILY PRODUCTIVITY REPORT shown below.

DAILY PRODUCTIVITY REPORT

Table 1

Standards Number of pieces packed per day	Unsatisfactory	Conditional	Satisfactory	Superior	Outstanding
	245 and below	246 to 289	290 to 347	348 to 405	406 and above

Table 2

Initials of the packer	A.S.	S.B.	B.D.	L.M.	J.C.	R.N.	B.G.	C.A.	D.F.	E.R.
Number of Pieces Packed Per Day	252	335	276	342	409	290	235	309	246	425

1. The number of packers whose productivity is *Outstanding* is   1.___
    A. 4   B. 3   C. 2   D. 1

2. The number of packers who come under the *Conditional* productivity standard is   2.___
    A. 1   B. 2   C. 3   D. 4

3. The percentage of packers whose productivity can be rated *Satisfactory* or higher is   3.___
    A. 30%   B. 40%   C. 50%   D. 60%

4. If every packer's daily productivity increased by 20 pieces, the number of packers whose productivity ratings would change to the NEXT standard is   4.___
    A. 4   B. 5   C. 6   D. 7

5. Which one of the following is an ACCURATE statement that can be made based on the information shown in Tables 1 and 2? 5.____

    A. There are more packers whose productivity is above the maximum Satisfactory level than below the minimum Satisfactory level.
    B. There are more packers whose productivity is in the Satisfactory standard than in any one of the other four standards.
    C. The number of packers whose productivity is Unsatisfactory is equal to the number of packers whose productivity is Outstanding.
    D. There is at least one packer whose productivity is in each of the five standards.

KEY (CORRECT ANSWERS)

1. C
2. C
3. D
4. A
5. B

TEST 6

Questions 1-4.

DIRECTIONS: Questions 1 through 4 are to be answered on the basis of the information given in the inventory tables shown below. Table 1 shows the amount of each item in stock according to the information contained on the perpetual inventory card for that item. Table 2 shows the amount of the same item in stock according to an inventory just completed by the staff.

Table 1

Perpetual Inventory Card	
Item No.	Amount of Stock
A107	2,564
A257	10,365
A342	7,018
A475	52,475
B026	16,207
B422	4,520
B717	21,431
B802	308
C328	594
C329	164
C438	723
C527	844

Table 2

Inventory Just Completed By Staff	
Item No.	Amount of Stock
A107	2,545
A257	10,356
A342	7,018
A475	52,475
B026	16,207
B422	4,505
B717	21,413
B802	308
C328	594
C329	143
C438	723
C527	854

1. In which one of the following items is there a difference between the amount of stock shown on the perpetual inventory card and in the inventory just completed?
   Item No.

   A. A257   B. B026   C. C328   D. C438

2. In which one of the following items is the difference GREATEST between the amount of stock shown on the perpetual inventory card and in the inventory just completed?
   Item No.

   A. A107   B. B422   C. B717   D. C329

3. The amount of stock shown for Item No. C527 on the inventory taken by the staff is greater than the amount shown on the perpetual inventory card.
   Of the following, the LEAST likely reason for this difference is that the

   A. perpetual inventory card was not brought up to date
   B. staff did not take an accurate inventory
   C. information entered on the perpetual inventory card was inaccurate
   D. staff made an inventory on the wrong item

4. Which one of the following is an ACCURATE statement that can be made based on the information shown in Tables 1 and 2?

   A. More than half of the items listed show a difference between the amount of stock shown on the perpetual inventory card and in the inventory just completed.
   B. One-third of the items listed show the amount of stock on the perpetual inventory card and in the inventory just completed to be 10,000 or more.

C. Less than half of the items listed show a difference between the amount of stock shown on the perpetual inventory card and in the inventory just completed.
D. One-third of the items listed show the amount of stock on the perpetual inventory card and in the inventory just completed to be 10,000 or less.

KEY (CORRECT ANSWERS)

1. A
2. D
3. D
4. B

TEST 7

Questions 1-3.

DIRECTIONS: Questions 1 through 3 are to be answered on the basis of the information given in the chart below.

ITEM NUMBER TOTALS AS OF JANUARY 31, 2009

Item No.	Monthly Usage	Current Inventory	Time Required Between Ordering & Delivery of Item
1	460	1,000	1 month
2	475	1,500	2 months
3	225	1,500	4 months
4	500	2,500	5 months
5	1,150	1,950	2 months
6	775	4,700	5 months
7	850	1,700	2 months
8	900	3,600	3 months
9	175	525	2 months
10	1,325	5,300	3 months
11	225	900	4 months
12	425	1,500	1 month

1. Which one of the following, if not ordered by February 1, 2009, would cause the monthly usage to exceed the current inventory before new merchandise could be received?
   Item No.

   A. 1   B. 4   C. 6   D. 10

2. Which one of the following must be ordered immediately because the current inventory cannot cover the monthly usage?
   Item No.

   A. 2   B. 3   C. 5   D. 12

3. The date by which Item Numbers 8, 9, and 10 must be ordered so that the monthly usage does NOT exceed the current inventory is _____, 2009.

   A. February 1   B. March 1
   C. April 1   D. May 1

KEY (CORRECT ANSWERS)

1. B
2. C
3. B

www.ingramcontent.com/pod-product-compliance
Lightning Source LLC
Chambersburg PA
CBHW082211300426
44117CB00016B/2764